HOW TO DO RESEARCH

Second edition

Nick Moore

The Library Association
London

© Nick Moore, 1987

Published by
Library Association Publishing Ltd
7 Ridgmount Street
London WC1E 7AE

First published 1987

British Library Cataloguing in Publication Data

Moore, Nick
    How to do research.—2nd ed.
    1. Research—Methodology
    I. Title
    001.4'2   Q180.55.M4

    ISBN 0–85365–787–4

Typeset in 10/12 pt Palatino by Input Typesetting Ltd,
London SW19 8DR.
Printed and made in Great Britain by Dotesios Printers Ltd,
Bradford-on-Avon, Wiltshire.

Contents

Preface to the second edition

This book has been written to provide practical help and guidance to anyone undertaking research. Many of the examples are drawn from library and information work simply because that is the field with which I am most familiar. The principles on which the book is based, however, are generally applicable and the guidance should be relevant to anyone contemplating social research or projects involving the study of organizations.

Having been involved with research in a number of roles – commissioning, conducting and consuming the end results – I have become increasingly convinced that in most cases what is required is a clearly focused objective, uncomplicated methods and clear presentation of results. In this book I have tried to provide some guidance on how such research can be conducted.

I have often been asked what makes a good researcher and what sort of training researchers should receive. In answer to this, I can do no better than to quote some remarks recently made by John Martyn, a most experienced researcher, who said:

> What makes a good researcher is firstly a total determination to keep to the deadlines in the project, secondly a decent respect for the tax payers' money that he or she lives on, thirdly a desire to do something genuinely useful as opposed to merely interesting, fourthly a combination of objectivity, a legalistic view of what constitutes evidence, a mind open to

vii

different interpretations of what the evidence may mean and a lot of imagination, fifthly a degree of numeracy, sixthly the ability to write up the results clearly, concisely and preferably amusingly, and seventhly a well-developed awareness that most people, especially researchers, have got it wrong most of the time. Good researchers should also never kid themselves that their findings are going to set even the most modest Thames on fire. Some of these qualities are innate and some can be taught. One or two, like being wrong most of the time, only come with experience, if ever.

The book could not have been written without the experience gained when I worked for the British Library Research and Development Department. Those four and a half years provided an opportunity to look at numerous proposals and projects and to become personally involved in some of them. I had plenty of opportunities to discuss all aspects of research with my colleagues, researchers and the consumers of research. My very grateful thanks go to them all.

More than just thanks should go to Elaine who gave me valuable comments and advice.

Nick Moore

1

State the objective of the research

The need for a research project to have a clear objective cannot be over-stressed. It is the key to the success of the whole venture.

A clear objective provides the basis for the design of the project, for the selection of the most appropriate methods and for the management of the project once it has begun. The objective is also the key factor in giving shape and purpose to the final report. Without a clear objective a research project can easily start on the wrong foot, become side-tracked along the way and end with an inconclusive report. During the process the researchers face confusion, uncertainty and the horrible nagging feeling that somehow they are missing the point of it all.

Research is a process which is almost impossible to define. There is a great deal of mystique about it and a reluctance on the part of many to consider undertaking it. It can cover a wide range of studies, from simple description and investigation to the construction of sophisticated experiments.

Seldom are social research projects repeated or duplicated, so every project tends to be different, yet they make use of a fairly limited range of techniques and methods which can be applied in differing circumstances. The basic skill lies in selecting the most appropriate methods for the task in hand. It is possible to build on experience and to learn from past mistakes but each project is different and requires a fresh approach.

The other main characteristic of research projects is that they are self-contained entities having a life of their own. Once the project has begun it is very difficult to slow things down or to speed them up. It is often impossible to go back and repeat something or to try it again a different way. Once the ball starts rolling it develops a momentum of its own. A clear objective should at least ensure that the ball begins travelling in the right direction and gives the researcher a fair chance of keeping it on course.

Before the objective can be specified, it is necessary to define what the problem is, and before that can be done there must be a clear understanding of why the research is being considered.

Research is carried out for two main reasons: as a means to an end, or as an end in itself. Both are perfectly valid, but each entails a rather different approach to the definition of the problem at hand and to the formulation of objectives.

Research as a means to an end

Here it is a question of looking at both the subject and the nature of the problem. The subject determines the location and operational constraints on the project; the nature of the problem governs the way it is approached. For example, it is possible to identify the opening hours of a library as the subject of research but it is impossible to go any further until the nature of the problem concerning the opening hours is specified.

It may be a specific problem which requires a solution. This would be the case if it proved necessary to reduce the opening hours of the service. In this case the research problem might be to determine a pattern of opening which would bring about the reductions required at minimum inconvenience to the users. It would then be possible to begin designing a project along those lines. Alternatively, the problem might be to reduce the opening hours by the required amount so as to bring about the greatest savings in staff costs. This would give a very different research project.

Solving specific problems is one of the most common tasks which the researcher is called upon to perform, but for the researcher it presents the most difficult projects. Problems are seldom simple and usually have many dimensions; there is a need to work quickly and to produce results upon which action can be taken and it is necessary to keep the scale of the research in tune with the size of the problem.

Information is often required, not so much to solve a specific problem as simply to remove uncertainty, or to increase knowledge or understanding. In our example, the researcher might be called upon to establish whether the existing pattern of opening hours adequately meets the needs of the users. The problem lacks the urgency associated with solving immediate difficulties and allows more scope for wide-ranging research.

The opening-hours projects provide fairly concrete examples of what might be termed investigative research projects. Frequently the research is concerned with much more nebulous questions, such as the perennial problem of measuring the effectiveness of the service offered or identifying users needs. In such cases it is often necessary to develop and apply techniques which have been produced elsewhere. The first task of the researcher is to look at the ways in which other people have tackled the problem and to determine whether or not what works in one context would work in another.

Market research falls into this category. Here the research is concerned to reduce the level of uncertainty about what it is that the users, and non-users, would like to receive from the service.

A completely different form of research is that which might be called experimental. This is probably closest to the popular stereotype of research as being something which takes place with rats or test tubes in a laboratory. The research is concerned with establishing what would happen if a change was made to the existing arrangements or if something completely new was introduced. It is possible to construct a model which can be used for tests but it is much more common to bring about the change, perhaps doing it in only one part of the system, and to measure what happens.

It is, for example, possible to speculate on the impact of a new pattern of opening hours, it is even possible to undertake some market research, but the actual result will never be known

3

until the new hours are introduced and their impact measured, and perhaps compared with another part of the system where no change has taken place. Similarly, it is possible to predict the comparative effectiveness of doing something – introducing two different patterns of opening hours would be a case in point – but again it is only possible to be certain by doing it in different ways and measuring the comparative performance.

Very closely related to this is research which seeks to establish whether it is possible to achieve something, or to bring about a change in something, by adopting a given course of action. For example, it is frequently stated that inflexible attitudes on the part of staff present the major barrier to the implementation of change; it has been suggested that it would be possible to change attitudes, or at least make staff more receptive to change, by means of training programmes. The only way to prove this would be to set up the training programmes and to see what happens.

Each of these problems calls for a different approach. It is quite possible that they will use the same methods, but the approach and overall design will differ. So it is extremely important to be clear about the nature of the problem and the precise reason why the research is being carried out. In this context the researcher is advised to look at the motives of those calling for the research because this will also condition the type of project to be designed. In addition to the problem-solving and uncertainty-removing motives, research is sometimes carried out as a means of education, either for the subjects of the research, the general public, or for a higher level of authority. It is often carried out as a means of delaying action or a decision, either in the hope that the problem will go away or in the expectation that the research will produce some evidence to support an unpleasant or unpopular course of action. Finally, there is the magical or mystical motive, where research is commissioned to give respectability to something or, more crudely, to mislead.

Before embarking on research as the means to an end, it is wise to be absolutely sure where the end is and what it involves.

Research as an end in itself

This type of research is more straightforward. The motive is usually clear – to obtain an academic or professional qualification, or simply for the satisfaction of the researcher – and will be reinforced by a general desire to increase knowledge and understanding, or at least to reduce the area of uncertainty. This type of research can, however, be divided into two main categories. There is research which is primarily based on a detailed and analytical review of the work of others. This is the type of work which usually leads to a Master's level qualification. The research is concerned with identifying relevant work and thoughts, submitting them to some form of analysis and synthesis in order to arrive at a clearer understanding, or to prove an hypothesis. The work may well be supplemented by a survey of some description, but in essence it is concerned with arriving at conclusions by reordering the thoughts of others.

The next stage up the academic ladder is the type of original research which leads to a PhD. Traditionally, Master's degrees were seen as a form of training for this more rigorous activity. As with Master's degrees, the project will build on the work of others and in this way will lead to the formulation of one or more hypotheses which are then tested by means of original research. In this way the research is expected to break new ground, develop new techniques or explore previously uncharted areas. The difference is one of degree.

Both types of research call for careful preparation. A crucial factor determining the success or failure of the work is the scope of the project and the range to be covered. Usually it is necessary to refine an initial idea down to something which is manageable. There should be sufficient literature on the subject to provide the basis for the research, but not so much that it is impossible to handle it within the time allowed.

It may be necessary to take account of the historical dimension of the project, perhaps going back to original source documents. This can be time-consuming and should not be underestimated.

A careful literature search should reveal the existence of other, related work, which needs to be taken into account. Full use should be made of indexes and abstracts. It is worth also checking registers of research, and contacting researchers or research bodies which are known to have a particular interest in the subject.

Rather different, but equally important, consideration should be given to the requirements of the institution for which the research is being carried out, and particularly to the likely level of help and supervision which will be forthcoming. In many ways academic research is a joint effort of the researcher and the supervisor, the latter playing a crucial role as a sounding-board for ideas, a guide to other relevant work and, most important of all, as a source of fair, informed and constructive criticism. A prospective research student should evaluate a potential host institution in these terms, and should be prepared to go elsewhere, or at least to modify the research ideas if the institution and the potential supervisor seem unlikely to suit the research project as originally envisaged.

Establish the objective

After the initial period of familiarization with the problem, its subject scope, nature and the motives which underlie it, the researcher is in a position to formulate the objective. It is worth repeating that this is an extremely important stage in the process and any temptation to hurry matters should be resisted.

The thing to look for is the essential element of the project – the one thing which characterizes it, distinguishes it from all other work and which encompasses the essential thrust of the project. This should become apparent after answering some basic questions:

- What is the project trying to achieve?
- What are the important issues?
- Who will be affected by the project?
- Who will benefit?
- What things will change?
- Why has the project been established?
- What kind of research is required?

Let us take as an example the problem which was referred to earlier – the scope for bringing about lasting changes in attitude by means of training programmes. Taking each of these questions in turn, it is possible to say that what we are trying to find out is whether or not training programmes can produce lasting changes in attitudes which will make the staff more receptive to change. The important issues are the very fact that attitudes can produce resistance to change; the nature of the attitudes themselves and their durability; and the extent to which training programmes can change the attitudes. An implied issue is concerned with cost-effectiveness – it is no good using training programmes which would be beyond the reach of the organization.

Finally, it is possible to say that some form of experimental research will be called for to set up the training programmes, to operate them and to measure their effect.

The objective now is to encompass all of this in one clear, unambiguous sentence which will fully express the essential element of the research. Such a sentence might be:

> The objective of the research is to test whether or not libraries and information units can use training programmes to bring about lasting changes in staff attitudes and in this way reduce their resistance to change.

If it is not possible to express the objective in this way then certain other questions should be asked:

- Does the project attempt to achieve too much?
- Is it too complicated?
- Do the people involved know what they are doing?

It is quite possible that what is really involved is not one but two or three projects which have been amalgamated. If this is the case then they may need to be separated in order to make the research manageable.

Having settled on the objective which will provide the overall direction for the project, it is now possible to break things down into more manageable tasks or activities. These then become the aims of the project and provide the basis for selecting methods, deciding on a work programme, managing the project once it has begun and ordering the results.

The aims can simply be a disaggregation of the objective – a

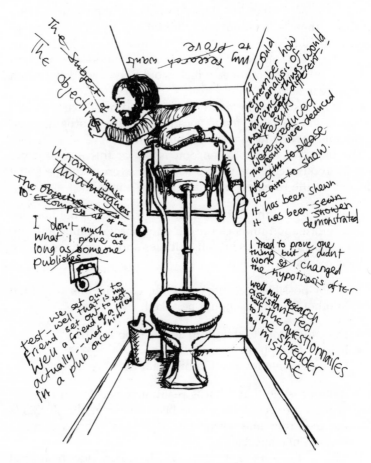

'. . . one clear, unambiguous sentence.'

division of the overall thrust into finite elements. In our example these might be:

- The preparation of training programmes
- The development of attitude tests
- The experiment itself, involving
  - an initial attitude test
  - the post-training attitude test
  - the later follow-up test
- The preparation of the final report
- The dissemination of the results, including the development of a training manual.

Another approach which is often adopted is to break the overall task down into chronological steps. This often produces very similar results to those obtained from disaggregation by the elements of the project. In some cases, however, different tasks will be taking place at the same time, and a chronological breakdown would only be confusing.

The shape of the research project should, by now, be clear and it is possible to begin thinking about the methods to be used, the time and resources required and the likely problems and critical points which will arise.

From here on things get easier.

2

Select the best methods

Research methods are no more than the tools of the trade. There is an unfortunate tendency to think that research begins and ends with research methodology. This is just not so. It is important to be aware of the range of research methods available and to understand how they work, appreciating their advantages and disadvantages. Such knowledge is, however, of little use unless it can be applied to specific research problems. The essential thing is to be able to select the method which is most likely to meet the objective of the research.

In general, one should beware of researchers who collect research methods like others collect stamps and who tend to regard each research project as an opportunity to add another method to their collection. Equally dangerous are the researchers who are totally committed to a single method – usually one which they have devised themselves – and who try to apply it to each and every problem.

The range of basic research methods is relatively small and it is not difficult to obtain a general understanding of them all. Each method does, however, have a number of variations or sophistications, which can be adapted to suit different purposes. In most cases it is sufficient to be aware of the existence of such subtleties, learning about the detailed application as each is called for by different research projects.

Many people are hesitant about embarking on a research

project because of the apparent complexity of the methods used in some research projects, particularly the use of sophisticated statistical techniques. Such people should not be deterred. It is possible to learn from experience and to begin research with only a partial knowledge of research methods. The secret is to keep things simple and to build on all the available expertise. Everyone finds it difficult to design their first questionnaire, for example, and most would benefit from some advice or assistance from a more experienced researcher. It is often the case that the second questionnaire is no easier than the first – simply because the pitfalls and problems are more evident – but from then on things become progressively more simple and straightforward.

One other thing about research methods is that it is possible to combine them to give added dimensions to the research project. For example, a postal questionnaire could provide a wide range of answers to any given set of questions but, because of the nature of postal questionnaires, these answers will tend to be rather superficial. This can be overcome by supplementing the questionnaire with some in-depth interviews of a smaller sample. In this way it is possible to give the research the required scope and depth without resorting to the very costly interviewing of large numbers of people.

Questionnaires and interviews are both types of survey. Surveys are probably the most common form of research method and they will be dealt with first in this chapter.

The primary function of surveys is to collect information which can then be analysed to produce conclusions. In order, however, to evaluate different survey methods it is necessary first to look at the purposes to which the information will be put. These are taken from an excellent book on social surveys by Godfrey Gardner called *Social surveys for social planners* (Milton Keynes, Open University Press, 1978) which can be recommended to anyone planning to embark on a survey. Another very practical source of assistance is a series of small guides produced by the Centre for Research on User Studies at the University of Sheffield. These guides cover:

- Designing a user study: general research design

- Basic social research techniques
- Analysing data
- Writing research reports
- Questionnaires
- Interviews
- Observation
- Group decision techniques
- Community profiling
- Group interviews

Together they provide much useful assistance, particularly for relatively inexperienced researchers (copies of the guides can be obtained from the Centre for Research on User Studies, University of Sheffield)

The first purpose of surveys is to describe what is going on; to obtain all the relevant facts about something; and to state those facts quantitatively. More sophisticated descriptive surveys may try to identify areas where problems occur or where changes are required, others may seek to measure the extent and nature of known problems.

In addition to explaining past change, surveys can be used to predict future changes. The changes may be beyond the control of the surveyor in which case the survey seeks to isolate the magnitude, nature and timing of the change. Alternatively, the surveyor may be in control of the change, in which case the survey is more likely to be concerned with predicting the outcomes of the change or examining the merits of different policy options. Once changes have been made, the surveyor may be called upon to evaluate the results of the change, perhaps even suggesting further changes which might be necessary.

From this it is possible to see that surveys are very flexible and widely used research methods. Given a small amount of common sense they can be used by relatively inexperienced researchers to produce useful results.

Observation surveys
The simple process of observing and recording events or situations is probably the oldest form of research. It is a research method, however, which is often overlooked.

There is a great deal which can be learned by careful observation of the world around us. Natural history, for example, owes much to scientists who observed, recorded and then classified what they saw. In social science, different techniques have been developed to improve our ability to notice what is going on and to record it in a form suitable for analysis; these will be dealt with later. Before then, it is worth noting that very informal observation can be useful during the early stages of planning a research project. When trying to identify the precise nature of a problem, it is often very useful to take a step back and look carefully at what is going on – at the way people make use of the service, or at the way staff operate different systems. A period of observation at this stage often clarifies matters considerably and usually proves useful when considering the most appropriate methods to be used and when thinking about the constraints which will be placed on the operation of different methods. If, for example, it is proposed to interview the users of a service, a brief period of observation will show where is the best place for the interviews to be carried out. It may seem obvious but it is small things like this which are often overlooked and yet which contribute towards the success or failure of the project.

More formal observation techniques are used when observation actually forms one of the methods used in a research project. Broadly, the techniques can be divided into participant observation and non-participant observation.

One form of participant observation is suggested by Robert Townsend in his book *Up the organisation* (London, Michael Joseph, 1971) when he says: 'Call yourself up. When you are off on a business trip or a vacation, pretend you are a customer. Telephone some part of your organisation and ask for help. You'll run into some real horror shows. . . Then try calling yourself up and see what indignities you have built into your own defences.'

Participant observation is thus concerned with putting yourself in the place of the client or user and seeing what happens. It is a technique which has been used to study the performance of reference libraries. Tom Childers did most to develop the method with his unobtrusive tests of American public libraries (Childers, T. and Crowley, T., *Information sciences in public libraries*, Metuchan, Scarecrow Press, 1971). In essence, the research involved posing as library users and asking a number of questions at different reference libraries. The results were usually extremely revealing.

The extent to which it is necessary to formalize participant observation obviously depends on the circumstances. If, for example, the objective was to test the accuracy of reference libraries' answers to questions, then it would be important to make sure that identical questions were asked by similar people in a very similar way and that the answers were recorded with some precision. It is also necessary to decide whether or not you are going to let the people who you are observing know that you are conducting research. Overt participant observation is when the subjects of the research are informed that they are being observed. Covert observation is what takes place when they do not know.

In non-participant observation, the researcher remains detached from the activity under observation and simply watches and records what is going on. It is a method which has been used for studying the patterns of behaviour in shops, for examining the preferences of people for different display techniques and it has often been used to record traffic patterns within buildings.

Advantages
Observation is a relatively straightforward method and, when combined with a little common sense, requires little training or familiarization. It provides the researcher with direct experience of a service, either through very close observation or through being on the receiving end. Such direct experience frequently leads to useful insights into the problem being researched and other peripheral matters. Finally it avoids the sort of bias from respondents which other research methods introduce. As far as possible, the client is undisturbed and it is possible to record undistorted behaviour.

Disadvantages
The main problem is that it can be very time-consuming. All research is labour-intensive and some methods are more so than

others. Unless there is a fairly constant level of activity, there is a danger that the observer spends much time simply waiting for something to happen. In other cases, so much might be happening that the observer is unable to see it all or, more usually, is unable to record it all. In such circumstances it is sometimes possible to overcome the problem by some form of sampling, otherwise it is necessary to increase the number of observers. This can produce another problem – if there are too many observers, or if the observer is too obtrusive, the people being observed may begin to behave differently. Reference library staff, for example, might become suspicious if a succession of people came into the library and asked the same set of questions. No one likes to be watched and we all modify our behaviour accordingly; this can significantly reduce the usefulness of the results.

A more serious limitation of the method is that it can only give a superficial impression of the problem. It may be possible to show that reference libraries give wrong answers to some questions but it will give few clues about why they do. It may be, for example, that the information in the reference books was itself inaccurate. To overcome such problems, some observers tend to draw inferences from what they observe. This is to be avoided if at all possible. That said, the line between observation and inference is a fine one and it is usually necessary to introduce a degree of inference, or interpretation, in order to record what is going on. For example, if someone in a reference library receives an answer to a question, smiles, thanks the librarian and says 'You have been most kind', it is reasonable to infer that the user was satisfied with the service which was received? Or should the observer try to allow for the fact that the user was dissatisfied but very polite and attempt simply to record the sequence of events as they occurred?

It is apparent that the recording of the observed events is critical and the manner in which they are set down often determines the extent to which they can be analysed. Unless some consistent recording format is used, much of the value of the information is lost.

Hints on using observation methods

The first thing to do is to make sure that everyone is clear about what it is that they are looking for. Once the process gets going there will be many things to look at and to notice, much that will seem at the time to be relevant to the study. Unless some clear guidelines are drawn up it is possible to end up with a great deal of useless information concealing whatever it was that was being looked for.

The second thing to do is to work out an economical way of recording the information. This should be in a form which can be handled easily by the observer who will need to be able to note down things quickly, but accurately. It should also be possible to transfer the observers' information into a form which can be used for analysis. It is not wise to rely on an ability to read the handwriting of someone trying to note things down under pressure. Where possible, the observer should simply have to tick boxes or circle numbers corresponding to the things observed.

Allied to this is the need to process the information as the research develops. Not only will this help to build up a picture, and thus help to identify critical areas, but it will also avoid the highly undesirable situation where the researcher is faced with the enormous task of analysing a mass of barely legible observation forms containing much information which earlier processing might have shown to be unnecessary.

Finally, if you are using covert participant observation, that is, your subjects do not realize that you are a researcher, it is always worth planning in advance how to get out of the situation of your cover is blown. There was, for example, a covert participant observation study carried out in America to find out what happens to patients who are involuntarily committed to mental hospitals. The researcher displayed unusual behaviour patterns and was committed. It then took him nearly a year to get out as the doctors believed that his claims to be a researcher were merely part of his illness.

Questionnaire surveys
Questionnaire surveys are probably the most commonly used and misused research method. Questionnaires are extremely flexible and can be used to gather information on almost any topic from large or small numbers of people. Questionnaire surveys do, however, have their problems. It is not easy to design a really good questionnaire and even well-designed ones

16

do not always manage to produce a high rate of response. Many of the problems can be overcome relatively easily, and some hints on how to do this are given below. First, however, it is worth looking at the two main forms of questionnaire and the uses to which they are put.

The commonest types of questionnaire are those which have what are known as closed questions. Here the respondent is asked a question and required to answer by choosing between a number of alternatives, hence the other name sometimes given to these questionnaire – multiple-choice questionnaires. The main advantages of this type are that they are easy to complete and easy to analyse. They provide a range of answers and thus reduce the chances of the respondent overlooking something and they reduce the possibility of obtaining ambiguous answers.

Closed questionnaires can only really be used to obtain fairly straightforward, uncomplicated information. When it comes to collecting information about differing shades of opinion, the format of multiple-choice questions ceases to be appropriate. Similarly, problems arise both for the respondent and the analyst when a question calls for a combination of answers.

The usual format for questions in this type of questionnaire is to ask the question then provide the range of answers, asking the respondent to tick the appropriate box.

How did you travel to the library?
On foot ☐
By car ☐
By bus ☐
Other (please specify) . . . ☐

This asks a simple question, presents a number of choices and should be easy to complete. Note that it includes a safety net in the form of the final response, just in case anyone flew or came by train.

The style of question given above does not, however, cater for the person who drove from home to the town, took a bus from the outskirts to the centre and then walked from there. Such a person would be better suited by a slightly different way of presenting the same question.

How did you travel to the library today?
On foot   Yes/No
By car   Yes/No
By bus   Yes/No
Other (please specify). . .

It would now be easy for this user to answer the question but it would be more difficult to analyse the answer. Things would get more complicated still if the questionnaire asked how the user usually came to the library. In this way it is possible to see how even a simple question can have several dimensions and how presenting a limited range of choices might produce an answer which is easy to analyse but which reveals only part of the whole story.

In some instances a simple 'yes' or 'no' response is not adequate. The question may be trying to get at shades of opinion or at strengths of preference. In such circumstances it is possible to use a rating scale.

Please indicate how you feel about different parts of the library service

	Very satisfied	Satisfied	Dissatisfied	Very dissatisfied
Lending service	☐	☐	☐	☐
Reference service	☐	☐	☐	☐
Short-loan collection	☐	☐	☐	☐

This provides more scope for the respondent to express an opinion but retains a sufficient amount of control to ensure that the information is capable of being analysed. One thing which should be remembered when planning questionnaires of this type is that some people have a tendency when answering questions to err consistently on one side or another, usually expressing greater satisfaction than they do in fact feel. This is generally known as a response set. It is possible to overcome this to an extent when setting out the questionnaire by ensuring that 'satisfied' or 'good' does not always appear on the left-hand side of the range or that some of the questions are expressed in a negative way. This will break up any pattern of answers but will not overcome any tendency to conform, which simply must be allowed for when interpreting the results.

To overcome some of these problems, many people use the other main type of questionnaire – one having open questions. Here the onus is placed on the respondent, who is expected to formulate and record answers in his or her own words. This has obvious limitations. It is only effective when used by people who are happy expressing themselves in writing and doing so succinctly. It produces a wide range of answers which are often very difficult to categorize and thus to analyse. It does little to ensure that potentially valid answers are not overlooked. Finally, it requires more effort from the respondent and is thus less likely to be completed.

Despite these limitations, open questionnaires can, under the right conditions, produce quite detailed answers to complex problems. They are most effective when used to survey a relatively small group of people who are used to expressing themselves in writing, who have a particular interest in the subject of the survey and who are likely to have reasonably similar opinions on the matter.

It is, of course, quite possible to devise questionnaires which combine both open and closed questions, according to the nature of the subject. Indeed, it is often desirable to follow a closed question with an open one to obtain any additional and relevant information. In nearly all cases, it is worth ending a questionnaire with an open question to obtain the respondent's general opinion.

Are there any further points you would like to make about travel to the library? ....
....

Always remember to leave enough space for the answer to be written in.

Advantages of questionnaires
Some of the advantages have already been mentioned. Questionnaires are cheap, relatively flexible and can be used to reach

a very large number of people. They can be designed to provide a degree of anonymity or to enable the researcher to follow up certain points at another time.

The questions are all presented in a consistent format and style and there is little scope for bias to be introduced by different researchers. Linked to this is the fact that the survey is impersonal and avoids some of the problems which can develop during the interaction between an interviewer and a respondent. The questionnaire can also be completed at the respondents' own pace, and the respondents can, if so desired, look through the whole questionnaire before committing themselves to anything – this avoids the problem of respondents beginning an interview by answering in a very defensive way.

Disadvantages

Again the main disadvantages have been covered – the lack of qualitative depth to the answers and the resulting superficiality, in particular. The method also allows for very little development or amendment as a result of lessons learned in the early stages of the research. For this reason it is extremely important to pre-test and pilot-test questionnaires, not only to ensure that the questions are unambiguous and answerable but also to check that nothing has been overlooked.

When gathering information by means of interviews it is possible to probe beneath an initially superficial response. This is just not possible with questionnaires. Even if it is possible to approach the respondents at a later date, the spontaneity will be lost. On a more basic level it is not usually possible to verify what appears to be an inaccurate response.

Hints on using questionnaires

The golden rule is to keep things short and simple. Prepare an initial draft and expect to reduce it in length by at least 50%.

Once the number, range and scope of questions have been decided, the next step is to set them out in the format which is most likely to reflect the true nature of the question, to be understood by the respondent and to produce answers in a format which can be handled by the researcher. This means that questionnaires have to be written in plain English. There

'The golden rule is to keep things short and simple.'

is a very good manual on writing plain English by Chrissie Maher and Martin Cutts, *Writing plain English: a guide for writers and designers of official forms, leaflets, letters, labels and agreements* (Manchester, Plain English Campaign, 1980). This should be required reading for everyone compiling questionnaires. Producing something in plain English is not easy. It is a time-consuming process and involves considerable attention to detail in both the wording and the overall layout and design of the questionnaire. It is, however, well worth it. A well-designed questionnaire will help to achieve a good response rate and will do much to create a good impression. The basic rules to bear in mind are:

Get the beginning right. Catch the interest of the respondent. State concisely what the survey is about and how they will benefit by completing the questionnaire. Give them an indication of how long it will take to complete the questionnaire.

Make it personal but unpatronizing. Write as if you are talking to the respondent. Aim for a warm, friendly tone.

Use simple words. Choose the sort of words which are learnt early in life. 'Form', for example, is a better word than 'Questionnaire'. Use words which have been derived from Anglo-Saxon rather than those which come from Latin or Greek. As a general rule, when faced with two possible words, choose the shorter one.

Keep the sentences short. Sentence length should vary but should seldom exceed 20 words. Use a different sentence for each main idea or significant piece of information. Resist the temptation to shorten sentences by leaving out words like 'a', 'the' and 'that'. In the notes and definitions, keep the paragraphs short.

Keep sentence construction simple. Try to follow the usual English word order of subject, verb and object (if there is one). Avoid having more than two clauses in a sentence. Use the active form of the verb – it sounds much better than saying, for example, 'the active form of the verb should be used'.

Use basic punctuation. In questionnaires it should seldom be necessary to use anything other than commas and full stops.

Use a large enough type size. If possible have the questionnaire typeset. Insist on a type size which can be read easily. Leave enough space for answers to be written in.

Avoid block capitals. It helps to ask respondents to write essential information in block capitals but it will not help them if the questionnaire uses them. People read by recognizing the shape of words. Using block capitals slows down the process.

Make it look attractive. Be a little fussy and aim for perfection. If possible consult a typesetter or graphic-designer. Use space generously and avoid a cramped, cluttered appearance.

These are good general rules, which are worth following in any writing. When designing questionnaires it is also important to avoid introducing bias into the questions. Rephrase any question which looks as if it might encourage a particular response, or which appears to express an opinion. Also avoid emotive words. The following are all examples of the sort of thing to avoid:

- Should librarians accept responsibility for maintaining cultural and educational standards?
- Should librarians be allowed to censor books?
- Would you like the opening hours to be increased?
- Do you think the present opening hours can be justified?

The other thing to avoid is ambiguity. This can sometimes arise from the use of specialized vocabulary, and in case of doubt it is worth giving a definition. In other instances it can arise through the construction of a question. This often happens when questions contain negatives.

Don't you think that opening hours should not be reduced?

Finally, ambiguity may be introduced by simple carelessness, or perhaps an over-active sense of humour – like the Government questionnaire which asked for details of 'employees broken down by age and sex'.

When planning the overall structure of the questionnaire, it is often worth arranging the questions so that they run from general to specific. This provides an opportunity for respondents to become familiar with the topic and to refine their ideas slowly. As a general rule, all the respondents should be able to answer all the questions. This is not always possible, however, and it usually helps to group questions that are relevant to only some of the respondents and to use a filter question to direct the others to the next relevant section. For example:

Have you used the reference library during the last month?   Yes/No
  – If **Yes** proceed to question 2
  – If **No** skip the next five questions and proceed directly to question 7

To help the respondent skip the right number of questions, it often helps to put a box around the questions to be jumped or to indicate question 7 with an arrow.

It is often necessary to add notes and definitions to qualify questions or to avoid ambiguity. Where possible, place the note or definition immediately below, or alongside, the question to which it refers. This can, however, lead to a very bulky questionnaire and to unnecessary duplication, in which case place all the notes and definitions in a separate section and provide clear instructions about consulting them. Arrange the notes in the same order as the questions.

Wherever possible try to maintain a constant style for responses. If some questions call for a tick to be placed in a box, and others for 'Yes' or 'No' to be deleted, errors are likely to creep in. Always leave room for an 'Other' response at the end of multiple-choice questions; it is usually worth asking the respondent to specify what the 'Other' signifies. Similarly, with many 'Yes/No' answers it is necessary to make provision for a 'Don't know' response. It is worth noting here that the 'Don't know' answer should not be automatically discounted – it may mean that the respondent cannot understand the question is ignorant about the subject and does not wish to express an opinion, is indifferent or simply unable to decide one way or another. Any of these responses could be significant.

When using multiple-choice questions it is well worth trying to make the choices mutually exclusive. This might result in a long list, in which case it is probably worth sub-dividing the question or grouping some of the categories. It is generally the case that analysing the results becomes difficult if there are more than ten responses to any single question.

The way in which the results are analysed will condition the design of the questionnaire. Before finalising matters try to work out in advance how the information will be analysed.

The first question to ask is whether you are going to analyse the results yourself, manually, or whether you are going to use a computer. With the growth in the number of microcomputers it is increasingly common to analyse survey results by computer. While this can save some time with the actual manipulation of the data, the use of a computer carries its own costs. It is, for example, necessary first of all to design the analytical framework within which the results will be processed. There are software packages for analysing data; alternatively it is possible to use normal spreadsheet programs, which are available for nearly all microcomputers. In either case, however, it is necessary to think through how the data will appear and what sort of tables are going to be required. Then it is necessary to input the data to the computer. This can be exceedingly time-consuming and in many cases the input time outweighs the other speed advantages of the computer.

Even when the data have been put into the computer, the analysis involves more than simply pressing a button. Computers are incredibly stupid things and tend to grind to a halt at the first sign of any imperfection in the data. Either that or they go berserk and start churning out thousands of correlations which seem to have little relevance for anything.

I recommend using a computer only as a very last resort and then only to process very large amounts of straightforward information. A much more satisfactory approach is to analyse the data manually. In this way it is possible to avoid the tiresome process of inputting, making it possible to begin by analysing only what is most essential and then developing from there. There is also a less tangible benefit. By handling the questionnaires, sifting through them and abstracting the data from them, one develops a very close understanding of what they contain and a feeling for the results which is seldom possible when using a computer. It may not be possible to produce quite so many correlations but it is almost certainly the case that the researcher will end up by understanding what is going on more clearly.

If a computer is to be used, then it is almost essential to consult the computing staff to find out what requirements they have for coding, or for the transfer of information from the questionnaire to a form in which it can be used as input to the computer. Even if manual analysis is planned it is necessary to give some thought to the analysis stage.

Try to think through how the questionnaire will be handled. Think about the number that will be returned and whether or not they will all come back at once or in stages, allowing the work to be spread. Think about the sort of tables to be drawn up. Decide what sort of correlations will be required; for example, will it be necessary to correlate or sub-divide the information by age or sex of the respondents? In a user survey it might be desirable to correlate frequency of use with distance travelled to the library, if so it will be necessary to ensure that both questions are asked and that it will be easy to transfer the required information from the questionnaires. Having done all this, go through the questionnaire again and consider whether all the questions are really necessary.

The administration of the questionnaire also needs some consideration. There are four main stages in addition to the preparation and analysis – pre-test, pilot, distribute and chase. Pre-testing is done at an early stage and simply involves sending a draft to someone who can be trusted to give an honest but constructively critical opinion. The second draft can then be used for a pilot. Pilot testing involves administering the questionnaire to a few respondents to check that it is likely to produce the information required without presenting problems. This is a stage which is frequently overlooked but it should not be. After any necessary redrafting, the questionnaire can be reproduced and distributed. It is worth contacting a few of the respondents just to make sure that they have received their copies.

Every questionnaire should have clear details of the date by which it is to be returned, and the address to which it should be sent (there should also be a telephone number for people who want to clarify anything). This will ensure that many are returned. There will, however, still be a need to chase up some later repondents. A polite letter is usually sufficient, enclosing another copy of the questionnaire in case the first one was lost. A telephone call is even better. It is unlikely that a second reminder will improve a response rate to any great extent.

One good way to improve the response rate is to offer respondents a summary of the results when the research is completed. This is not an unreasonable thing to do – after all you are asking them to do you a favour – and it does help to produce a high response rate.

It may seem that the compilation of questionnaires is so complicated and subject to pitfalls that it should not be attempted by novices. This is not really the case. It is simply that once the questionnaire is distributed it is on its own. It has to be self explanatory and compete with a wide range of other things which may seem more important to the respondent. Careful prior thought and preparation ensures that it stands the best possible chance of being successful.

Interview surveys

Interview surveys have a great deal in common with questionnaire surveys. The large-scale interviewing exercises such as public opinion polls are really no more than questionnaires administered in person. They require an interview schedule which needs to be designed in much the same way as a questionnaire. This type of survey is known as the structured interview survey. Rather less formal, but still placing heavy reliance on the interview schedule is the semi-structured interview. A third type of interview survey is becoming increasingly popular: this is the in-depth interview, where a few people are subjected to a detailed, and inevitably less structured, encounter. Such interviews often more closely resemble a discussion of the subject in hand than an attempt by one person to obtain information from another. Finally, there are group discussions.

Structured interviews are built around a questionnaire. Instead of the questions being read by the respondent, they are asked by a surveyor who also records the answers. The surveys are carried out like this for a number of reasons, the main one being that it allows the researcher greater control over the sample of respondents. Sampling will be dealt with later, but suffice it to say that in some instances, such as political opinion polls, it is vitally important that the sample statistically represents the population being surveyed. If self-completion questionnaires were used, almost inevitably some people would not respond and the researcher could never be certain that the non-respondents were representative of the whole group. There would always be the chance that the non-respondents were so opposed to the subject being surveyed that they refused to participate. If the questionnaire is being administered by an interviewer, they can carry on until a fully representative sample has been questioned.

The other main advantage of interviews is that even with a highly structured interview schedule they provide an opportunity to obtain qualified answers. This is done in two ways – by probing and prompting. Probing is when the interviewer asks the respondent to explain an answer in a little more depth. If, for example, a respondent says that they only used a service after trying all other possibilities, the interviewer could probe by simply asking why. When planning structured interviews, particularly those using a number of interviewers, it is necessary to make clear which questions are to be probed and in which way.

Prompting, on the other hand, is an attempt to ensure that the respondent has considered all possibilities when replying to the question. It is usual for the interviewer to pose the question, wait for the answer and then say something like 'Have you ever considered any of these. . .?' The interviewer then either reads out a list of alternatives or hands over a card on which they are printed. Again the questions which require prompts and the timing of the prompts need careful specification in the interview schedule.

Semi-structured interviews provide much more scope for the discussion and recording of respondents' opinions and views. The interview schedule still needs to be carefully designed but it will consist of some fairly specific questions, each of which may be probed or prompted, and a number which are completely open-ended. These latter questions mainly serve as a check list for the interviewer to ensure that the question is asked, that different facets are explored and that all the possible answers are covered. Semi-structured interviews are used to collect discursive information – qualitative as opposed to quantitative, to use the jargon – which usually contains a high degree of opinion or the expression of attitudes. It is a technique that could be used to explore such things as the type of service that people want, or the nature of problems experienced by managers. The interviews require a degree of structure but should, none the less, be fairly free-ranging.

The less structure there is to an interview the more effort needs to be put into ensuring that the interviewer stays fairly close to the point and is not drawn into interesting but irrelevant side-issues; that they record the information in an objective and consistent manner; and that they cover all aspects of the problem. This obviously presents much less of a problem if the interviews are conducted by one person who can usually be relied upon to maintain a fair degree of consistency. Where a number of interviewers are used the schedule should contain clear and precise instructions and there should be a period of training to help everyone at least to begin in the same way.

The next stage in interview surveys is the in-depth interview. The objective of these is to collect complex information, containing a high proportion of opinion, attitude and personal experience. As a technique, it differs only in degree from semi-structured interviews. The objective is usually to set up an interview in which the respondent is prepared to discuss at length a subject which is of equal interest to them and to the interviewer. It is almost essential to build up trust in order to arrive at the truth of matters which are frequently quite sensitive.

Some would claim that only the most experienced researchers should undertake interviews of this kind and, because of their complexity and the need to keep discussions moving in the right direction, this is usually the case. The exception is when the subject of the interview is well known to the interviewer who can then discuss matters with confidence and weigh up responses, probing those which do not seem to fit.

It is partly for this reason – the need to understand the topic – that in-depth interviews are often preceded by a more general information-gathering exercise, which provides the necessary background and from which it is possible to identify critical areas which can then be pursued in greater depth. Once the interviews begin, new insights will develop and, because the structure is flexible, these can be used to enhance later discussions.

Group discussions are, quite simply, interviews carried out with a group of people rather than with individuals. Because a group is more difficult to handle than a single individual, it is usually necessary to have a fairly clear idea of the structure which you hope the discussion will follow. Equally, however, it is impossible to adhere to a very firm structure, as the main advantage of group discussions is that they provide an opportunity for matters to be discussed in depth, with one person's views sparking off feelings and attitudes among others in the group. The task of the interviewer when conducting group discussions is difficult, as it is necessary not only to ask the questions, to ensure that all the matters are covered and that the responses are recorded but also to ensure that all members of the group participate equally and that no single individual dominates. As with all other forms of interviews, of course it is necessary to do all of this without expressing your own views and opinions or leading the group in any way.

Even though group discussions can be difficult, they should not be ignored as they can produce a very detailed, in-depth understanding of particular issues and can provide a depth of analysis which is seldom possible in other ways.

Advantages of interview surveys

As has been noted above, the first big advantage of interview surveys is that they make it possible to achieve a complete response with different categories of a sample, and thus ensure the statistical validity of the results (assuming the sample itself is statistically valid, of course). The second is that it is possible to collect more complex information, where necessary, qualifying answers and generally obtaining results with a greater 'depth'.

In addition, interviews are more personal than questionnaires and tend, therefore, to produce better response rates. They provide the researcher with more control of the survey, making it possible to collect information at precise times, perhaps spreading the collection over a fairly lengthy period to see whether there are any seasonal fluctuations. The interviewer also has much more control over the flow and sequence of questions. It is sometimes important to ask a particular question after others have been answered – with questionnaires it is impossible to prevent respondents looking ahead to see what is coming.

Finally, it is possible to make the survey much more responsive to early results. If there is a limited amount of analysis taking place as the results come in, it is possible to add to the schedule to explore any interesting issues that have come to light. This is obviously less possible with the more structured interviews.

Disadvantages of interview surveys

The main disadvantage of interview surveys is that the information obtained is often difficult to analyse. It may be possible to use quantitative methods for some of it, but the method will probably have been chosen to collect information which, by its very nature, is not susceptible to this form of analysis. Even the highly structured opinion polls tend to produce information which does not sit happily within the confines of a statistical table and which calls for narrative discussion. Some of the ways of overcoming the problem will be covered in the section on analysing the information, in Chapter 6.

The other main problem is that of ensuring a high degree of consistency in the presentation of the interview. Trained interviewers can overcome many of the problems associated with bias: becoming too personally involved with the interview, or simply the wearing experience of coming into direct contact with a large number of strangers every day. For the part-time researcher the problem is not so easy to overcome. Much can be done by only a few individuals, but, even so, it is difficult to be sure that the results are not influenced in some way by the interviewer.

Hints on using interview surveys

Many of the hints given for questionnaire surveys apply here. The schedules need to be very carefully designed and further thought has to be given to how the question will sound when spoken. The introductory statement needs to be clear and to convey the function and purpose of the survey in such a way that it will encourage the respondent to agree to participate. The early questions should be easy to answer and should aim to put the respondent at ease. Any contentious or difficult questions should be about half way through, at the point when some rapport has been established and before boredom sets in. At the end of the interview, the interviewer needs to check that all the questions have been fully answered, so it is necessary to build in a signing-off paragraph, perhaps asking the respondent if they have any points which they would like to raise or if they have any questions. While they are thinking about this the interviewer can do a quick check to see that all is complete.

Instructions for the interviewer should be clear and unambiguous. It should be clear that some passages and questions are to be read as written, while others may be phrased in a variety of ways to suit the situation. Similarly, the instructions about probing and prompting should be clear. It is useful to indicate whether or not a 'Don't know' response should be probed. This calls for clearly laid out interview schedules which make it easy to distinguish between questions and instructions. There is nothing worse than asking something which turns out to be an instruction to the interviewer, or missing a question because you thought it was simply a note.

The form should be so designed that the interviewer can record the information while the interview takes place. This calls for boxes which can be ticked, or numbered responses which can be circled. With semi-structured and in-depth interviews, there is a temptation to tape record the proceedings rather than to take notes. Aside from the fact that a tape recorder introduces a note of artificiality into any interview, the danger is that few notes will be taken and some poor typist will be handed a batch of tape cassettes and asked to produce transcripts. Anyone contemplating this is well advised to record an interview then have a go at transcribing it themselves before they inflict it on anyone else. If a tape recording is felt to be essential it is probably best to play it through as soon as possible after the interview and take detailed notes from it then. Above all else, avoid the situation which all too frequently arises where the researcher at the end of the interviewing phase tries to make sense of a couple of hundred pages of transcribed interview. Semi-structured or not, the task is daunting.

The exception arises with group discussions. During the discussion the researcher will be fully occupied asking questions, ensuring that all the ramifications are explored and endeavouring to get the person at the back to say something this time. It is unrealistic to expect the researcher to record the results of the discussion at the same time. Here a tape recorder is essential. It is, however, almost impossible to obtain a full transcription of a group discussion. Not only does everyone interrupt every one else but it is usually impossible for someone who has not participated in the discussion to identify different voices consistently. The solution is for the researcher to play the tape back as soon as possible after the discussion and to make detailed notes at that time.

When carrying out the interviews, try to be pleasant but not pushy; objective but not detached, and relaxed but not so laid back that the interview is punctuated with long pauses. Do not be too eager to note down responses, particularly 'Don't know'; many responses begin 'I don't know . . . well yes, I suppose I would say that as a "Don't know" '. Above all else, avoid getting into long theoretical discussions about the subject being surveyed, or worse, feeling the need to put the other side of the argument.

Sampling

Sampling is an essential aspect of surveying. It is seldom possible to survey the complete population. Population in this context means all the people or objects under observation. A sample is a group selected from the complete population, to make the task of surveying less costly, and more manageable. The secret is to select a sample that will represent, or have the same characteristics as, the overall population. More precisely, the chance of a particular characteristic or attribute occurring in the sample should be the same as the chance of the same characteristic appearing in the whole population. This can be achieved by selecting a random sample, by, perhaps, selecting every tenth unit or by giving each member of the population a sequential number then selecting from a table of random numbers.

The size of the sample can be varied to give different degrees of accuracy. In this case, accuracy is measured by the standard error, this being the percentage variation, plus or minus. Thus a result of a sample survey which gave 70% for and 30% against with a standard error of 5 would mean that in the population as a whole anything between 65% and 75% would be in favour (70% plus or minus 5 percentage points) and between 25% and 35% would be against 30% or minus 5 percentage points). The standard error does not depend simply on the size of the sample, although these will be important. The standard error actually depends on the nature of the responses to different questions, and each question will therefore be subject to a different standard error. In some reports, statistics are given quoting this standard error factor.

All in all, the statistical aspects of sampling can become complicated quite rapidly, and an inexperienced researcher uncertain about an acceptable sample size is well advised to consult a statistician.

It is sometimes advisable to introduce an element of structure into the sample rather than basing it entirely upon a random selection. In general, this is applicable when the population being surveyed is composed of more than one identifiable group, each of which is likely to have markedly different characteristics. An example of this is to be found in the case of public reference library bookstocks. In Britain there are more than 500 reference libraries of a reasonable size, yet over 80% of all the reference books in the country are concentrated in fewer than ten large city reference libraries. These large collections are likely to have characteristics which may not be found in the smaller libraries. It is therefore necessary, in selecting a sample of British reference libraries, to structure or stratify the population by dividing it into the ten really large libraries and the rest. The actual sample is then drawn randomly from each of the two groups. In this particular case it will probably be necessary to take a 100% sample of the ten large libraries.

Opinion polls work in a similar way. The researchers divide the population into homogeneous groups, each of which is likely to have characteristics which differ from the others. The interviewers are then required to interview a specified number from each group. The resulting samples are called quota samples to distinguish them from stratified samples as they are not ranomly selected in the true sense – the interviewer selects from the people who happen to pass by in the street or wherever the survey takes place. In this sense the sample is self selecting.

The design of a sample and the actual random selection are very important particularly with quantitative surveys where the results should be expressed with a high degree of precision. It is very easy for inexperienced researchers to make mistakes which could invalidate the whole process. It is wise, therefore, to consult a statistician for expert advice.

Experimental research

This is the traditional type of research used by scientists. The researcher sets up an experiment in order to test an hypothesis or theory. The experiment is usually designed so that the researcher has as much control as possible over the conditions under which the actual tests take place. For this reason most scientific experiments take place in laboratories. Researchers in social organizations do not face many problems which are amenable to laboratory testing in this way, although some research into, for example, the comprehensibility of forms and leaflets has taken place in a type of laboratory. None the less, experimental research methods can be used for a fairly wide range of problems.

The starting point for any piece of experimental research is an hypothesis. This is usually in the form of a proposition or theory about the relationship between two different elements of the overall system. An example would be the hypothesis that higher levels of duplication of popular books in a library will reduce waiting lists for those books. The objective of the experiment would be to establish whether or not the hypothesis is valid.

The two elements under examination – duplication levels and waiting lists – are called variables. The proposition is that waiting lists depend on levels of duplication, so the waiting lists are called the dependent variable and duplication levels are known as the independent variable. An experiment sets out to vary the value of the independent variable and to measure any resulting change in the dependent variable. In the example given, therefore, the researcher would probably select a random sample of popular books and measure the levels of duplication and the length of the waiting lists at the beginning of the research. The levels of duplication would then be increased and at the end of the research period the length of the waiting list would again be measured to see whether there had been any change. Simple measurements are thus used to see whether there is any relationship between dependent and independent variables.

If such an experiment had taken place in a laboratory where all the other variables – the size of the collection, duplication levels of other books, the demand for material and so on – had been kept constant, the experiment might have produced some useful results. However, in the real world it is simply not possible to be sure that all other variables remain unchanged and therefore have no influence on the result. To help overcome this, researchers use a control group. This is a group or sample which has the same characteristics as the experimental group, but which is not subjected to any change in the independent variable. By comparing the results of the control group and the experimental group it is possible to have more confidence in the results.

This type of research is known as the four-cell experimental design.

	Value of dependent variable before treatment	Value of dependent variable after treatment
Control group		
Experimental group		

The values in the two left-hand boxes should be the same at the beginning of the research because the two groups, or samples, will have the same characteristics. Only the experimental group will be subjected to changes in the value of the independent variable and it is therefore reasonable to assume that any differences in the values in the two right-hand boxes will be attributable to the changes made to the independent variable, in which case the hypothesis is valid.

Things are not quite as simple as this. For example, simply because the value of the dependent variable changed it does not mean that there is a causal relationship between the two. It may be that the independent variable affects an as yet unidentified variable which in turn affects the dependent variable. Just because two things vary in the same way does not mean that there is any direct relationship between them – it has been said that there is a strong positive correlation between the rise in the use of ball-point pens and the increase in juvenile delinquency, but we would be unwise to assume that there is any relationship between the two.

Despite the need to interpret results with caution, experimental research can be used to great effect in certain circumstances. A case in point is the research which was used as an example in Chapter 1 – testing the hypothesis that lasting changes in staff attitudes can be brought about by training programmes. It would be necessary to make use of a four-cell experimental design to test this hypothesis.

First it would be necessary to select at random two samples of staff. One group would become the control group, the other the experimental group. At the beginning of the research each group would receive tests to establish their attitudes at the outset of the study (the values in the two left-hand boxes). The experimental group would then receive training programmes specifically designed to change attitudes. It would be necessary to make sure that, as nearly as possible, all other factors remained unchanged. At the end of the training period, both groups would again receive the attitude tests to give the values in the right-hand boxes. Any difference in attitudes could reasonably be assumed to have something to do with attitude-change training programmes. To test the durability of the change, a further attitude test could be given to both groups after an appropriate amount of time had elapsed.

If it could be shown that training programmes could bring about changes in attitude, further experiments could be set up to test the effectiveness of different types of training. The basic design would be the same.

Advantages of experimental research

Most organizations are complex and relatively little is known about the way in which they operate, the internal dynamics and the relationship between the parts which make up the overall system. In the past individuals have developed theories and acted upon them, introducing changes and modifications which have often improved the efficient running of the organizations but which occasionally have proved to be somewhat less than successful. By experimenting it is possible to establish the validity of theories before taking positive action on them. This not only saves time, effort and resources, but in many cases the experiment can throw light on important aspects which need to be understood if the theory is to be fully exploited.

In short, experiments enable ideas to be tested in a controlled way without jeopardizing the smooth running of the overall system.

Disadvantages of experimental research

The principal disadvantage is that it can lend an air of spurious accuracy to the research results. Because the conclusions are the product of what may well have been a period of intensive research, there is a tendency to accept them at face value. In the real world, however, many factors can influence the course of the research and even the most painstaking research design will never be able to eliminate the influence of every variable. It is necessary, therefore, to treat the results with some caution. In scientific research it is normal practice to repeat the experiment a number of times to establish the consistency of the results. This seldom happens with social research, partly because of the nature of the experiments, and consequently it is not possible to place such a high degree of trust in the results.

One common reason for the results of experimental research to be distorted is what is known as the Hawthorne effect. This is a phenomenon observed at the Hawthorne works of the Western Electric Company in the 1920s and 1930s. They were looking at different incentive schemes for assembly line workers and eventually discovered that increased productivity did not depend on any particular incentive but on the workers thinking that, by introducing an incentive, management was taking an interest in them. In a research context it has been found that changes occur in a control group simply because they have been singled out as a group different from the rest. It is obviously rather difficult to avoid such a phenomenon and due allowance needs to be made when interpreting results.

Hints on conducting experimental research

Careful preparation is essential for this type of research. The design of the project, the selection of the sample and the measurement of the dependent variable are all crucial to the success of the research, and any errors here can invalidate the results. It is therefore wise to consult experienced researchers and statisticians and to plan with some precision.

It is particularly important to ensure that the control and experimental groups are comparable. This is largely a question of sampling and of ensuring that the samples are properly selected. Once selected it is important to handle both groups consistently. Usually the groups will not know which is the control group and which the experimental. Often the control group is not made aware of the existence of the experimental group.

The other critical thing to remember is to make sure that the independent variable is in fact the thing which is varied and that the dependent variable is measured accurately. There was, for example, an experimental research project which sought to test the hypothesis that placing books in a prime display location produced increased use (as measured by the number of times the books were borrowed). The study carefully selected 100 'good' books from a published book list, randomly selected two groups – one control and one experimental – of libraries and, in the experimental group, placed the books on display shelves next to the issue desk. In the control group, the books were left as normal on the shelves. The use of the books was carefully measured and at the end of the period it was found that the experimental group of books had been issued more frequently than those in the control libraries. From this it was deduced that prime display location did influence use. What was overlooked, however, was that the books selected were 'good' books and that the increase in use might have been due to the fact that the users' attention was drawn to these books. Had this been done in some other way, by means of a booklist or poster, for example, use might have increased in exactly the same way. If, on the other hand, the sample of books had been selected at random from the stock of the library, the results would have been more valid.

This simply shows the need for careful preparation and the importance of ensuring that all is what it seems.

Historical research
In contrast to experimental research which was developed in scientific disciplines, historical research is quite definitely a product of the humanities. Essentially it is an attempt to describe and to learn from the past. As such, it can be purely descriptive, recording the sequence of events and presenting the fullest possible picture of the development of something. The intention is to record and describe.

Other historical research sets out to prove an hypothesis. It does this by collecting and presenting evidence in such a way as to allow conclusions to be drawn and from these the hypothesis to be established or invalidated. There are relatively few good examples of this type of research.

Advantages and disadvantages of historical research

It is difficult to specify particular advantages or disadvantages of historical research, although it can be asserted with some confidence that, like motherhood and wholemeal bread, it is a 'good thing'. By looking at the past it is possible to put some of the problems of today into their proper context.

Hints on undertaking historical research

Organization is the key. It is easy to become overwhelmed by material and to lose sight of both the overall objective of the study and the significance of the document under consideration.

The first thing to do is ensure that the topic is of manageable proportions. The scope of the subject and the time span should be such that they involve the use of an appropriate amount of source material. This will obviously depend on the nature and intent of the research – a thesis prepared for a professional qualification or a Master's degree will obviously have greater scope and depth than an extended essay prepared as part of a taught Master's course. All of these will be less extensive than the major works which frequently draw on literally hundreds of documents.

In selecting and refining the subject of the research it is obviously important to take account of the amount of source material, its nature and its accessibility. It is probably more time-consuming to work from primary sources than from secondary, and due allowance should be made for the work of gaining access to the information. It may be necessary to allow for a period of fieldwork to permit access to documents in remote locations. At the same time non-printed sources should not be ignored. Questionnaires and interviews can both be used to obtain information from individuals, and increasingly there is a body of audiovisual recorded information, notably recorded interviews, broadcast programmes and films.

At an early stage in the research it is worth planning a systematic method for taking notes and recording information, and then fitting this into the overall scheme of the research. If material is not to be overlooked, it is necessary to develop some means of storing and retrieving relevant items.

Periodically during the research it is advisable to stand back from the immediate concerns of the study, to attempt to see the overall shape of the project. It will be important to see how much progress has been made, particularly if working to an externally-imposed timetable. It is also necessary periodically to re-assess the general direction of the research. It would be an unusual piece of work which did not alter course in some way as it developed. New insights will suggest different paths to follow or different approaches to the main idea of the work. There is, however, a danger of pursuing red herrings or being diverted up blind alleys. To avoid this, every opportunity should be taken to discuss the work with the supervisor, or with someone having a knowledge of the subject. They will be able to see the work in a clearer perspective and should be in a position to offer objective advice. For this reason, the choice of supervisor is particularly important.

Operational research
Operational research was developed during the Second World War to help military planners cope with large-scale logistical problems. Since then the techniques have been applied to a wide variety of organizations.

Basically, it involves the application of mathematical techniques and principles to organizational problems. The organizational researcher tries to understand the different forces and relationships which cause organizations to behave in the way that they do. Having understood what is going on, the next stage is to construct a model of the organization which can then be used to explore the different outcomes which would result from variations in the elements which make up the organization. The model is not made out of card and balsa wood like architect's models; instead it is built up using mathematical equations and established theories. In its final form, the model can be expressed as a series of equations which can be used to calculate quite precisely the dynamics of the organization.

The models begin with the most easily understood relationship, for example, the relationship between the rate of duplication of popular books and the length of the waiting lists for them. Starting from this base the researcher would then attempt to formulate the relationships between all the other factors which might have a bearing on the length of the waiting lists. These might include the availability of alternative books on similar subjects, the strength and urgency of the demand, and the fact that people are less likely to join a queue the longer it gets. Some of these relationships may already be expressed in mathematical terms – there is, for example, a well-established theory of queuing – others will need to be developed by the operational researcher to meet different circumstances.

Having expressed the dynamics of the organization in numerical terms the next task is to calibrate the model or, in other words, to use real values to 'tune' the model so that it reflects the changes which take place in the real world. For example, the basic model may express the relationship between duplication rates and the length of waiting lists in this way:

The length of waiting lists depends on the level of duplication, the higher the duplication rate, the shorter the waiting list.

This is fine for describing what is happening but it is not adequate when it comes to using the model for prediction. It is therefore necessary to collect information that will enable the researcher to state the relationship much more precisely, saying, perhaps, that every time the duplication rate is increased by a factor of two, i.e. doubled, the length of the waiting list will be reduced by a factor of four, or reduced to a quarter of its previous length. This calibration stage is extremely important in the production of models for precise forecasts or predictions. In other cases it may be enough to describe the general relationship and then let the knowledge of that guide decision-making.

One of the best-known examples of the application of operational research techniques to library and information problems took place in the late 1960s and early 1970s at Lancaster University. Michael Buckland described some of this work in his book *Book availability and the library user* (Oxford, Pergamon, 1975) which describes in some detail the research which was conducted into the relationship between loan periods, duplication levels and levels of demand. The whole programme of work demonstrates how it is possible to build up a clear picture of the ways in which a library works and to use this knowledge to improve the performance of the organization.

Advantages of operational research

Most researchers, particularly those who have carried out several projects, are well aware that the organizations they work in are complex and often unpredictable. Frequently there is only the haziest understanding of the different forces which are at play in determining the outcome of alternative courses of action. Operational research, by focusing on different elements of the organization, can do much to eliminate areas of confusion and generally increase the level of understanding.

It does this by throwing light on previously misunderstood relationships, often indicating the significance of factors which previously had been discounted. The research approach is also such that it presents the results in a way in which they can be used to improve the efficiency of the organization. Indeed, the whole ethos of operational research is directed towards action and towards making the results of past and future policies explicit.

The application of operational research frequently involves people who have had little or no previous connection with the running of the organization. This fact alone does much to clarify the minds of people who are often so concerned with day-to-day problems that they are unable to see the overall organization and the way in which it operates. Quite frequently, the process of explaining to an outsider how something works helps to clarify matters for the person doing the explaining or, at least, it serves to highlight just how much is not understood.

Disadvantages of operational research

Operational research works very well with relatively simple systems where it is possible to express relationships quite precisely, to calibrate using readily available information relating directly to the different elements of the system and to construct an understandable model which is sufficiently flexible to be used for a variety of purposes. This, however, is not always the case. Most social organizations have diffuse objectives, users who have a wide range of motives for using the service, an intangible product and elements which are often difficult to quantify. In such circumstances, it is possible to construct simplified models which can provide general guidance on the effects of different policies. To go beyond this, however, often means that the resulting model is very complex, making use of a large number of equations to express a wide variety of relationships, many of which interlock. In such circumstances, the application of the model becomes a complex task and the results, if they are not heavily qualified, are subject to fairly wide margins of error.

In view of this, many people have questioned the value of operational research, particularly as it often appears to involve long-winded methods to explain what many people think they have known all along. Much of this, however, is a problem of communicating with an expert from a different discipline and can be avoided if both parties approach the problem with open minds.

That being said, there are certain dangers associated with using outside experts. Such experts have their value but it is usually related closely to their area of expertise. Once they stray outside their area of expertise they frequently cause problems for all concerned. Consequently, operational researchers, in common with all other experts, should be used with care and, wherever possible, used in combination so that their operational research expertise can be informed by someone who has a thorough understanding of the organization under examination.

Hints on using operational research

As we have just noted, the process usually involves the combined efforts of researchers and those with direct operational experience. In this sense, it is important to find the best way of working with the researcher.

The crucial starting point is a full and precise brief. It is essential that the researcher understands the problem and the purposes to which the results will be put. Once this initial understanding is gained it will provide the basis for the future, more detailed, discussion of the ways in which the organization works. The researcher will then go away and will try to express the relationships mathematically, using analytical approaches which often resemble those of systems analysts. This done, the researcher and the person from the organization then need to work together again to specify and collect the information needed to calibrate the model. Once this calibration is done, the results need to be set out in a form which can be used for the purpose which was originally intended.

The end product of the whole process may be a report produced for wider distribution. Such reports often fail to make the impact which they deserve. It is probable that this is because the very nature of operational research and the use of models requires that the initial approach expresses things in very simple ways, gradually building in the sophistication which is found in the real world. Readers of such reports often fail to get beyond these early stages, having lost all confidence in an approach that appears to express in simplistic terms something which they know to be much more complicated. Either that, or they feel that, by explaining what goes on in simple terms, the report is adopting a patronizing tone.

All this has done little to encourage the application of operational research techniques, which is unfortunate. It is necessary to approach the reports and conclusions from the point of view of the operational researcher, beginning in a simple way and gradually enhancing the basic structure with the variations which occur in the real world. Such variations, however, would be of little value if the underlying assumptions proved to be false.

In short, a sympathetic approach and a willingness to participate in a joint effort are essential starting points.

Case studies
Case studies and the two methods which follow – evaluation and action research – are not so much research methods as

approaches to the whole business of research. They are included here, however, as they frequently provide the framework within which other methods are employed for specific purposes.

Case studies can be used for two purposes – either to reduce the scale of the research by focusing on fewer units or to increase the range of units within the study.

The first approach is similar to sampling, except that it would be unusual to look at more than about ten case studies. By selecting a number of case studies it is possible to concentrate the research resources and thus to look in some depth at a particular problem or issue, perhaps considering how it is treated in different circumstances. In such research, the case studies will be selected to be broadly representative of the large group from which they are drawn as much will depend on the degree to which it is possible to generalize from the particular results. Such an approach was adopted by the Library Advisers at the Department of Education and Science when they embarked on a study of the effects of expenditure reductions on public libraries. (Department of Education and Science, *Maintaining library services: a study in six counties*. Library Information Series No 8, London, HMSO, 1978). This study made use of two types of case study. First, six county libraries were selected for investigation. They were chosen not because they were representative of all authorities, but on the grounds that they would shed some light on general trends, while at the same time being sufficiently comparable to provide a basis for generalization. Second, within each of the county library services, three individual libraries were chosen for detailed surveying. In each county, there was one large, one medium-sized and one small library. Again these were not selected as samples in the strict sense but to indicate what was happening generally. These two-tier case studies provided the structure for a fairly wide-ranging investigation which made use of surveys, both questionnaire-based and interview-based, and some statistical analysis and interpretation of management information.

Case studies are usually used when the research is attempting to understand complex organization problems or the diffuse causes and effects of change. In essence it allows the researcher to focus on something which is sufficiently manageable to be understood in all its complexity.

Advantages of case studies
The resources available for research are always scarce and case studies provide a means of covering a large amount of ground for an acceptable cost. More particularly, they provide a means of looking in some depth at complex problems. By using case studies, it is possible to compare a number of different approaches to a problem in sufficient detail to draw out lessons which have general applicability.

Disadvantages of case studies
By their very nature, case studies are used to illustrate general points and to arrive at conclusions which can be generalized to cover a much larger number of situations. They lack, however, the statistical validity of samples that have been properly selected and therefore the extent to which valid generalizations can be made depends on both the degree to which the case studies themselves are typical and the care used in drawing conclusions. It is, therefore, very important, when looking at the results of research based on case studies, to pay particular attention to these two points.

Case studies are often used to illuminate complex processes, their outcomes and antecedents. This can be a time-consuming process and, particularly when looking at organizational change, the research can extend over months or years. The disadvantage of this is that the rest of the world does not wait for the publication of the research results and when they appear they have often been overtaken by events.

It has already been shown that the research process itself can distort events – the Hawthorne effect – and this is always a problem with case studies. With research which is concerned with organizational dynamics, it is almost impossible to avoid the research process having a significant impact on the course of events. The simple fact that researchers are asking questions about the ways in which things developed causes the respondents to think more carefully than they otherwise would, and this in turn is reflected in their subsequent behaviour. Indeed, there is a school of thought which would claim that this is one of the strengths of the case-study approach – that it alters peoples' perceptions of their work and thus causes them to adopt a more rational and systematic approach to the task in hand. In this way the research process itself helps to bring about the changes – research becomes an integral part of the change process.

Hints on using case studies

Setting up the research is crucial. Before any approach is made to the case studies, it is important to work out the extent to which the research will impinge on the day-to-day operations of the case studies and from this to consider how the inevitable interference can be minimized.

Some thought should also be given to the degree of neutrality which the researchers should adopt. If the case studies are being used for a simple investigation of a course of events, as was the case with the DES study cited earlier, there is a fairly clear demarcation line between the researchers and the practitioners. On the other hand, if the research is seen more as part of a longer term process of organizational development, with the research study not only illuminating the organizational dynamics but also contributing to the influences at work, then the division between researcher and practitioners becomes much less marked. If such considerations are not thought through before the research begins the whole relationship between the researcher and the practitioner may start on the wrong footing.

Having determined the scope and nature of the study, the next stage is to select the case studies and again this requires careful preparation. First it is necessary to be clear about whether the case studies have been chosen for their comparability or because they represent a range of alternatives. Then the formal approaches must be made, requesting permission to use the organization as the basis for research. This must make clear the contribution which will be expected and the likely benefits to be gained from participation. The fullest possible information at this stage will help to alleviate (or in some cases confirm) any suspicions in the minds of those being asked to participate.

Having obtained the co-operation of the case studies, the researcher must then establish an effective working relationship with those being researched. It has already been shown that the style of the relationship will differ with the nature of the research but, whatever style is adopted, the researcher will nearly always be faced with some initial suspicion, hostility and uncertainty on the part of the practitioners. At the very best, the suspicion will be tinged with some enthusiasm generated by the novelty of the experience; at worst, there may be hostility which can easily lead to a refusal to co-operate. In between, there is the general view that all this research nonsense is only marginally relevant to the pressing concerns of the real world. The first task of the researcher will be to overcome the hostility, dispel the suspicion and provide the practitioners with enough information to allow them to reassure themselves. The researcher must somehow become accepted by the practitioners as an equal; without that it will be almost impossible for them to collect any reliable information.

Having established a good working relationship, it will be necessary to ensure that this does not interfere with the objectivity of the work. Particular care must be taken to ensure that the information collected, and the interpretation of this information, does not become subject to bias or any especially favourable or unfavourable slants. This is not easy and there are no simple hints about how it can be achieved. It does require above all else, an ability on the part of the researcher to remain detached, no matter how amicable the relationship with the practitioners becomes.

Evaluation and performance measurement
For many years, researchers have been asked to attempt to evaluate newly introduced services, or alternative ways of delivering services, and to measure the performance of the organizations. Various research methods have been used, and a number of lessons have been learned. It is still, however, an area where there is a degree of confusion and uncertainty, and one in which much basic development work remains to be done.

Considerable confusion surrounds the forms of measurement

and the terminology used to describe them. There are really only three different concepts – the measurement of efficiency, the measurement of performance and the measurement of effectiveness.

Efficiency is concerned with how well the organization is performing. It is not concerned with the questions of whether or not a particular service is needed, or whether it is directed at the most appropriate client group; all that is being considered is whether the same level of service could be offered using fewer resources, or whether an increased level of service could be offered using existing resources.

Performance or *effectiveness* measurement, on the other hand, is concerned with measuring the extent to which a service or operation is achieving an objective. It is this objective that provides the yardstick against which the performance is assessed. It is quite possible for a service to operate at maximum efficiency yet for it to fail to meet its objective.

The measurement of *impact* attempts to assess the impact which a service has on its users, and looks at how it has fulfilled their expectations and satisfied their needs. So far, despite many efforts, no techniques have been devised for measuring *impact* in a cost-effective manner, although some pioneering work has been done.

There have been numerous projects making use of a wide variety of methods and techniques. The difficulty however, has always been that the output, or product, of most social organizations is intangible and therefore difficult to measure at the best of times. Things become really difficult when attempting to measure the impact of this intangible product on individual users. It is arguable that it is not really practicable to attempt to measure the impact of most social organizations simply because the problems involved are so intractable. People who put forward this argument point to the advertising and education industries, both of which have devoted considerable efforts to measuring the impact of their products, all to no avail.

Of more practical relevance is the evaluation of services which have been newly introduced, the comparative evaluation of different forms of service or operation and the measurement of

51

performance or success in achieving an objective. The starting point for any project of this kind is the objective of the service or organization. As with the type of objective discussed in Chapter 1 of this book, the overall objective can be broken down into a number of specific aims. Once these have all been established, the next stage is to develop performance indicators. This is often the most difficult step because the performance indicators must at the same time be easy to measure, and reflect the actual aim or objective.

An information service to small businessmen might, for example, have as one of its specific aims:

To communicate relevant current developments by means of seminars, conferences and workshops.

It would be possible to measure the performance of the service in this area by simply counting the number of seminars, conferences and workshops. This would only give part of the picture – the events might, after all, have been of such dismal quality that no one bothered to attend. To enrich the information it would, therefore, be wise to include a count of the number of people who attended and, perhaps, the number who attended more than one – on the grounds that if the event did not meet the participants' needs they would be unlikely to return. All of these measures would give an indication of the extent to which the service was meeting its objective and, what is more, they would be easy to collect. It would be possible to go further and to ask each of the participants to complete a questionnaire asking them for their reactions to the event which they have just attended. This would, however, be more costly and it might be felt to add little to what was already known.

This sort of performance measurement can relatively easily be built into organizations to provide a type of management information which is relevant to the different aspects of the organization. It is necessary, though, to make a conscious effort to link the measures to the objectives. It is all too easy to continue to collect statistics without really being aware of their purpose.

Measuring the performance of an existing service in this way is quite straightforward. Objectives are unlikely to change markedly from year to year although the targets, expressed in terms of the performance indicators, may well be varied. It is more difficult to evaluate a newly introduced service, or to undertake a comparative evaluation of alternative services.

The starting point for such an exercise would again be to establish a set of aims and objectives and to develop from these a range of performance indicators. In a comparative evaluation it will obviously be possible to compare the performance under each aim, and from this to arrive at a conclusion, making the necessary allowance for the fact that some aims will be more important than others. With a new service, it would be difficult to determine what level of performance is satisfactory. It would be possible to set targets but difficult to draw any firm conclusions about the performance of the service using these indicators alone. This problem would be faced, for example, by a public library which was introducing an on-line computerized information service. The objective of such a service might be:

> To provide rapid access to a wide range of bibliographical and other information.

Within this overall objective there would be a number of specific aims, one of which might be:

> To increase the range of published material read by library users.

The performance indicators for this aim could be the increase in the use of the library's reserve stock of little-used material, and the increase in the number of items borrowed from other libraries in response to demand. Both of these would provide crude indicators of performance but it would be difficult to attribute any changes to the introduction of the on-line service. In this case, the only effective way to measure the performance of the service in this respect would be to ask the users.

Having conducted a survey of the users, and perhaps having found that in half the cases the on-line service did lead the user to information which they would not otherwise have used, the librarian is faced with the problem of deciding whether or not this performance counts as being satisfactory. The expectation might have been that all users would have been alerted to additional sources, and to that extent the service has not come up to expectations, but then such an expectation might have been completely unrealistic in the first place.

The problem is a difficult one. It can be overcome partially by finding out what happens in other libraries which have on-line services, or by keeping an open mind about performance until a sufficient time has elapsed for the service to settle down and for comparative information to become available.

To evaluate the performance of a new service, or to compare two alternatives only gives part of the picture. It is important to look also at the efficiency of the services. It may be that the performance is such that it satisfactorily meets all the aims and objectives, but in doing so absorbs a disproportionate amount of resources. It will therefore be necessary in any evaluation to undertake an assessment of the efficiency of the operation of the service. This could be anything from simply recording the resources required by the service – mainly financial and staff time – to a complex efficiency audit using work measurement techniques. Whatever is chosen must be commensurate with the size of the problem.

Advantages of evaluation and performance measurement
The main advantage is that they provide decision makers with a basis for allocating resources in the way which is most likely to maximize their use and they allow the staff directly concerned with the service or operation to monitor their own performance and to look objectively at the work they do.

Without any evaluation or performance measurement there is a tendency for organizations to become choked with services and operations that have outlived their usefulness, that never performed as well as was hoped, or that consume resources which could be used to greater effect elsewhere. Performance measurement provides the necessary mechanism for taking the difficult decision to stop doing something that no one really needs any more. It also allow the organization to build on its successes. In all, it enables the organization to become and to remain relevant to the needs of its users.

The evaluation of new services and the comparative evaluation of alternative forms of service ensure that the organization does not begin to accumulate bits and pieces which, though they seemed good ideas at the time, it can ill afford.

Disadvantages of evaluation and performance measurement
There are not many disadvantages. There is a possible danger that an over-rigid application of such assessment could stifle the creativity of the staff whose job it is to develop and improve services and operations. There is also a possibility that new services will be unfavourably evaluated, and subsequently abandoned, before they have a chance to become fully established. Other than this there is little that can be said against either technique.

Hints on using evaluation and performance measurement
Implicit in what has just been said about the disadvantages of these two approaches is the need to interpret results with a degree of flexibility and in consultation with those directly concerned with the operation of the service, and the need to let new services become established before taking drastic decisions based on the evaluation.

It is also very important to establish the objective and aims quite clearly and to take some care when deciding upon the performance indicators. There is no substitute for common sense and the ability to think the whole matter through when it comes to this part of the overall project.

It is necessary to be realistic about the amount of information which should be collected about a service. As a general rule, the cost of collecting, processing and interpreting the information should seldom be more than 5% of the total cost of operating the service. Although when evaluating new services it is likely the proportion will be greater, as the decision whether or not to continue the service will be taken on the basis of the information gathered.

The subjective assessment of the people concerned with the day-to-day operation of the service should never be overlooked. Indeed, it is important to involve these staff in the evaluation or measurement process. They must be able to recognize that the evaluation process does not present a challenge to them and that the work does not involve an assessment of how they perform their tasks. The presentation of the work must make it clear that the results will benefit staff as much as anyone else. This has implications for the way in which the whole evaluation or measurement process is designed.

Finally, do not ignore the ultimate beneficiary – the user. Social organizations exist to meet the needs of their users and that must always be the ultimate criterion when assessing any form of service or operation. It therefore makes sense to go directly to the users to obtain an opinion. To do this by large-scale surveys is expensive but by sampling, or even by observing and simply talking to a number of users, perhaps using group discussions, it is possible to collect a great deal of valuable evaluative information.

Action research
Just as Molière's bourgeois gentilhomme was astonished to discover that he had been speaking prose for the previous forty years without knowing it, so many people are surprised to find out that for many years they have been conducting action research projects without being aware that they were doing anything half so grand.

At its simplest, action research involves setting something up and running it to see what happens. As such, most experimental research which takes place within social organizations, as opposed to laboratories, can be thought of as action research. It is necessary because in many situations the only way to establish the feasibility of an operation or the extent to which a service can meet a need, is by going ahead – by initiating the operation or establishing the service – and observing what happens.

In a strict sense, action research involves slightly more than this. To be properly regarded as action research a project would need to contain a continuous thread of objective evaluation and a mechanism whereby the results of the evaluation and the lessons learned during the project can be fed back into the process so that it becomes dynamic and constantly modified in the light of experience.

A good example of an action research project is the South Molton Community Information Project which was based in

Devon County Library Service and was funded by the British Library Research and Development Department. Previous research had shown that in rural areas people's needs for community information were often unsatisfied, and that where attempts were made to provide information and advice, services were often fragmented and poorly publicized. Devon County Library sought to overcome this in South Molton, a small market town on the southern edge of Exmoor, by using library accommodation to provide facilities for the complete range of information and advice agencies which operated sporadically from the town. In this way they hoped to introduce some benefits from shared facilities and, with luck, to encourage additional agencies to provide services.

Nothing like this had been tried before on such a scale and the only way to see whether it would work – whether all the organizational problems could be overcome, whether the facilities could effectively be shared and whether the library was the most appropriate focal point – was to set the thing up and see. The British Library provided funds for staff and some other expenses. They also provided a consultant who was able to follow the course of the development and to provide a degree of objective evaluation and assessment.

The project was established and after an initial period began to operate quite successfully. The consultant assisted with evaluation of the project, and a steering committee of experts otherwise unconnected with the project provided advice and some objectivity. Lessons learned were fed back into the operation of the service and, after a period of successful operation, conclusions were drawn and the experience made available to a wider audience by means of a report and a seminar. (David Venner and Sally Cotton, *Information for a rural community: the South Molton Community Information Project*, British Library LIR Report No. 40, 1986).

This was an almost classic piece of action research, having all the expected characteristics – clear prior evidence of need for the service; commitment on the part of those most closely involved with the day-to-day operation; continuous evaluation and monitoring; feedback of information into the operational design of the service; objective assessment from impartial experts; and dissemination of the results so that lessons learned could be made more widely available.

Advantages of action research

The main advantage is that it is real, concrete and everyone can see what is going on. This can have its disadvantages – the mistakes are that much more public – but on the whole it makes for a research project which has the support and backing of people who might otherwise be called upon to act on research results with which they were unfamiliar and, consequently, to which they had little commitment.

The other aspect of the concreteness of action research is that something exists at the end of the day. In other types of research, it may be possible to establish that something is needed, but actually bringing it about can take some time and considerable effort. There is always the chance that by the time things get going all the energy and enthusiasm which once existed could be dissipated. With a successful action research project the intervening stage is avoided and there can be a smooth transition from research to operation.

For the practitioner, action research imposes a discipline on developmental work which is often otherwise lacking. For the researcher it brings the real world into focus and makes the purpose of the activity all the more apparent.

Disadvantages of action research

The previous section noted that it can be embarrassing to make mistakes in public. It can also be damaging in the eyes of the ultimate controllers of the organization. To set up a service that is then shown to be inappropriate makes little political sense and could weaken the reputation of everyone concerned.

Action research which shows a service to be not worth continuing can also be frustrating for the users. It is unlikely that the service will be a failure in the eyes of all the users, and for those whose needs have been met it will be annoying to see the service withdrawn.

Hints on using action research

The objective of action research is to see how things will work in the real world. Due attention must, therefore, be paid to ensuring that the research process does not distort the operation of the service. The first thing to do is to make sure that the research process, particularly the evaluation, is kept as unobtrusive as possible. It is, for example, unrealistic to expect people to use a service naturally if they are constantly surrounded by researchers earnestly clutching clip-boards.

It is also important to make sure that elements of the service are not over-exaggerated simply because it is a research project. There is a common tendency, for example, to spend considerable amounts on publicity for the new service. This expenditure can sometimes be justified financially because it is a new service and one which is the subject of a research project, so it makes sense to ensure that as many people as possible know about it. However, if the publicity budget exceeds that which would normally be allocated to such a service, then much of the benefit gained from conducting the research in a real environment will be lost.

It is important to keep everyone involved in the service fully informed about every stage in the operation of the research and of the service itself. What must be avoided at all costs is the development of a barrier between the researchers and those actually operating the service. The researchers need to retain a considerable degree of objectivity but this need not detract from the sense of working in a team which is essential for the successful conduct of action research projects. Equally important is the need to keep the staff in the rest of the system informed about what is going on. It would be surprising if an action research project in one part of an organization did not spark off some suspicion in other parts of the organization. This must be overcome, if for no other reason than that the other staff may one day be given the job of developing services based on the lessons learned from the research. Regular communication can overcome many of these problems. But it must be *communication* – sending around a duplicated news-sheet is not enough.

The next point concerns action research projects which are

funded by external agencies. This is becoming increasingly common as budgets become more stretched and the funds available for development diminish. To ensure continuity, some allowance must be made for funding the service once the initial period of research support has ended. There can be few things more frustrating than to establish a service, prove its success, then wind it down because no arrangements have been made to secure adequate funding. This point is all too often overlooked and many people have been put in the position of scrabbling around for money to keep operational services in which they believe when they would be far better employed actually running the service. Fluctuations in the resources available to an organization will always occur and it is impossible to allow for every contingency; however, it is extremely important to think ahead and make the necessary provision as early as possible. This done, the people who control the resources should then be involved in the project and be encouraged to become committed to it so that when asked for the resources to continue, they know what they are buying.

Finally, strive to retain objectivity. Try hard to avoid becoming so committed to the service, or so fed up with it, that the selection of evidence artificially makes a case for or against. As has been said before, there is no easy way to do this. It is simply part of being a good researcher.

Selecting the best methods
For any project the possible range of research methods will be determined by the nature and scope of the problem being researched. Withing the overall boundaries, however, there is considerable room for manoeuvre and it is often difficult to settle on any single set of methods. To aid the selection of research methods, there are six common-sense principles which, if followed, should ensure that the project stands a reasonable chance of success.

Keep things simple
This principle should perhaps be written in full as: keep things simple – they will always get more complicated than you think.

Begin by adopting a simple and straightforward overall

'. . . keep things simple . . .'

design for the project. Reduce things to the bare essentials and concentrate most of your efforts on those. If you can get the basic structure right, many other things will follow from it. In that sense, good research is similar to good furniture design – functionalism, simplicity and the lack of unnecessary complexity are what distinguish the good from the bad.

Having established the overall design which focuses on the key issues, try to identify research methods which themselves are uncomplicated and which are within the competence of the people undertaking the research. It is no good deciding to use an operational research approach if no one in the research team has experience of mathematical modelling. In some cases, it may be possible to call upon outside experts for advice but you should not over-estimate the contribution such experts can make.

The methods should also be commensurate with the time available and the general scale of the subject of the research. There is little point in swamping a small service with a massive research project.

An important thing to question is the degree of accuracy which is required. Social organizations are, at their best, imprecise organisms which are subject to innumerable variables beyond the control of the researcher. In such circumstances, it is not realistic to employ highly sophisticated methods which produce results down to two decimal places. It is simply not worth aiming for such levels of accuracy in the results if the basic data is subject to wide margins of error. Equally, it is pointless to attempt to obtain high levels of precision if the people for whom you are undertaking the research simply want an overall, impressionistic view of the situation.

The simplicity can also be affected by the volume of data being collected. Large samples, lengthy questionnaires, detailed surveys and large amounts of data analysis will all inevitably contribute to the complexity of the research.

In many cases, it is worth considering whether what is known in the trade as a 'quick and dirty' review would be sufficient. These seldom claim to produce definitive answers but they are short, focused, can provide cost-effective answers and, more particularly, can be used to clear the ground ready for a more detailed project later. There is nothing intrinsically wrong with such projects, although many purist researchers may turn their noses up at them. It is simply a case of tailoring the research to meet the requirements of the situation.

In summary then, start the project as simply as possible and throughout the research keep asking if it is possible to simplify things still further. Concentrate on getting the essentials right and leaving the non-essentials to sort themselves out.

Borrow from others

One of the easiest ways to keep a research project simple is to borrow from other projects, learning from their mistakes and seeing where short cuts can be taken. At the beginning of this chapter, the point was made that research methods are like tools and, like any tool, they are not easy to design or invent, yet they can be used in a variety of conditions, and it is often possible to see how a small addition or alternative could fit them perfectly for the task in hand.

It is always worth looking around to see whether someone else had tackled a similar project. If so, the results may provide the answer required and thus obviate the need for further research. At the very least it will be possible to learn from the approach adopted. Often the techniques developed for other projects can be used directly. In particular, it is worth looking closely at questionnaires to see what can be adapted or built upon. The advantage of this is that it provides an opportunity to compare results with those obtained elsewhere.

It is also possible to transfer analytical techniques from one project to another and to build upon them. For some types of research, indeed, this approach is almost unavoidable. In the area of performance measurement, for example, different approaches and techniques have evolved over the years and questions should be asked about any performance measurement project which did not, to a certain degree at least, build on the work which had gone before.

Collect only what is really needed

This should be engraved on the forehead of every researcher. It is probable that more projects have come to grief because they collected too much information than for any other reason.

'Collect only what is needed'

Here it is necessary to distinguish between *wants* and *needs*. Some researchers seem to *want* an unlimited amount of information about the organizations they study and about the problems which the organizations face. They are actually *interested* in slightly less. They can *handle*, physically and mentally, much less. In reality they *need* only a very little.

The tendency is to think that our understanding of a problem will increase as we collect more and more information about it. In fact, the reverse is usually the case. It is possible to learn a great deal about something through detailed consideration of a little carefully chosen information which relates to key issues. When more questions are introduced, the amount of data increases but the understanding declines.

What should be avoided at all costs is the 'while we are about it . . .' syndrome. This is the phenomenon which exists when someone announces that they are about to undertake a survey. Before long, someone else comes along and says 'While you are about it, could you ask a question on. . .?' Before long, the questionnaire runs to 20 pages and its original purpose is lost in a mass of detail. The only thing that this will achieve is to ensure that the response rate is much lower than it would otherwise be.

It is also possible to collect too much information by failing to select small enough samples. The marginal increase in the accuracy of a sample diminishes quite markedly once the size of a sample goes beyond a certain point. A very large sample, therefore, may simply add to the burden of analysis without adding to your understanding or the accuracy of the results.

Significant problems can arise through the use of too many methods. In any single project, it is quite common to use more than one method in the expectation that the findings will complement each other. Care should be taken that this is, in fact, the result and that the methods do not simply overlap.

A further point to bear in mind is that the amount of information collected should be constrained by the capacity of the organization to process it and of the researcher to make sense of it. All over the world on the desks of researchers, there are large piles of transcripts of tape-recorded interviews which the researcher will get around to analysing one day, while in their cupboards there are stacks of computer printouts just waiting for the afternoon without interruptions.

Beware of the distortion which the research creates
Some research methods are more obtrusive than others and it is important to select methods which will minimize the amount of distortion which can occur. There was once a study which aimed to find out what happened when library users asked a question at an enquiry desk. The method of data-collection adopted was to hang a tape recorder around the neck of the user and one around the neck of the librarian. The researcher then told them to act naturally. . . .

It is impossible to avoid distortion altogether, although it is worth taking steps to reduce the effect. In most cases, it is simply necessary to accept that the distortion will occur and to make allowance for it in the conclusions.

Use available expertise
Some research methods require considerable skill and expertise if they are to be used successfully. When considering such methods it is always worth bringing in experts who can advise on the suitability of the methods, provide some basic training and assist during the project itself. It is, however, vitally important to establish a good working relationship. The involvement should be such that the detailed knowledge and experience of the method of the expert are shared with the librarian or information worker contributing the detailed understanding of the subject of the research. Without such a joint approach there is a danger that the expert will devote much effort to establishing facts which have been accepted by those 'in the know' for years.

Accept that some things cannot be measured
Far too much time has been spent in attempting to measure phenomena which cannot be measured. It is, for example, almost impossible to obtain a reliable measure of the impact of a service on an individual. The complexities and variables, to say nothing of the need to take time into account, mean that it is simply beyond our capacity to measure. We might obtain

'Beware of distortion . . .'

subjective judgements from individuals after they have received the service but how can you measure the impact six months later? In some cases, it is possible to obtain some form of measurement but the cost of doing so makes it extremely hard to justify the exercise.

Rather than continuing to chase the elusive goal of measuring things which cannot be measured, we should simply accept that certain things are beyond our grasp and, instead, we should rely on other approaches, such as the use of subjective judgements and surrogate measures.

Cost-benefit studies are classic examples of attempts to measure the unmeasurable. Nearly every cost-benefit study has a weak point, in that somewhere there will be a benefit on which it is impossible to place a cost.

If these six simple criteria are used to guide the selection of methods, there is a good chance that the project will be both cost-effective and within the competence of the research team.

3

Write the proposal

Just as a builder requires plans to guide and assist the building of a house, so a researcher needs a proposal to provide a structure for the research project. All too often the proposal is looked upon as an inconvenience, which is only required if external finance is sought for the research or if it is necessary to obtain the approval of an academic institution or professional association for research, leading to the award of a qualification. In fact, proposals can play extremely important roles in all research projects. It may seem wasteful to spend time preparing a proposal when the effort could be used to get on with the research, but the preparation of a proposal ensures that all aspects of the research are thoroughly thought through before the research itself begins. Once the research gets going it is often too late to make changes and adjustments which would have been obvious had there been adequate preparation.

The functions of research proposals
Research proposals have a variety of functions, some of which depend on such factors as whether external funding is sought. Each proposal needs to be tailored to meet the particular requirements of the research project, and obviously, small in-house projects call for a rather different approach from projects involving specially recruited staff and a major research grant.

As with so many things in research, it is a matter of common sense.

To aid planning

No matter what the scale or nature of a research project, the preparation of a proposal is an invaluable aid to the planning of the overall project. The discipline imposed by having to set down thoughts on paper ensures that all the stages are considered and allowance is made for every eventuality.

The proposal should put the research into context, making the researcher actively consider the events leading up to the work, the need for it and the relevance of other work in the area. This stage may well require some investigation of its own. It will almost certainly require a literature search to establish what else has been published, and a check of research registers for other relevant research which may be in progress. It is necessary to consider the need for the research and how it fits in with the overall development of the organization.

The proposal must contain the statement of the objective of the research and the specific aims which will be realized. If nothing else, the proposal should force researchers to set down these vital elements on paper.

A proposal should also cover the methods to be used. Again, the discipline of preparing the proposal ensures that there is a good chance that the different methods are fully considered and planned so as to be complementary and likely to achieve the objective of the research. Setting them down in this way will also make the people who will be carrying out the research consider whether they are happy with the methods chosen, or whether it will be necessary to call in some expert assistance.

The methods will determine the resources required for the project. Every proposal should contain some reference to resources and to the source of them, whether they will be required at an even flow during the course of the project, or whether there will be times when the flow will be larger than usual. For example, fieldwork is usually expensive and it usually takes place during the early part of the project, whereas analysis, interpretation and report preparation usually involve little more than salary costs, and take place towards the end of the project. There is thus a tendency for the expenditure to be greater at the beginning of the project than at the end. This can be critical if external funds are involved, as the funding agency will probably plan for a regular cash-flow and may be alarmed if early claims seem to be disproportionately high.

Allied to the methods and resources are the pattern of the work and the time required for its completion. It is not easy to ensure a consistent work flow and it is helpful if the proposal indicates the sequence of different tasks and both the time required and the elapsed time which will be necessary. For example, a questionnaire survey might require six weeks of a researcher's time – two on preparation and design, one on distribution, one on receipt and chasing and two for analysis. This will, however, take place over a much longer period as there will be times when no action is called for from the researcher – when the questionnaire is being piloted and when it is with the respondents being completed. It is therefore necessary to fit different activities in so that there are few slack times and no periods when everything needs to be done by next Tuesday. The proposal stage is the time to do planning of this sort and to decide upon an overall pattern of work. Details will inevitably change as the research progresses, but the overall shape should be decided in advance.

To guide the project

Once the research has begun, pressing day-to-day concerns can easily obscure its overall direction. A good proposal can prove invaluable at this stage as it helps to put things into context and should explain the relevance of different activities. The importance of this will obviously vary in direct proportion to the size of the research project. A project lasting two years and employing a small research team will obviously need detailed guidance if the overall momentum and direction are to be main- tained. Even on small projects, however, it is easy for the researcher to feel rather lost half-way through a project. In almost every piece of research there is a stage at which the researcher feels that the topic is too great to come to grips with but that the particular problem being studied is so insignificant that it is difficult to justify the research. This phenomenon

'. . . it is very easy to feel rather lost . . .'

occurs in just about every research project and you should not be alarmed when it happens to you. When this stage is reached it is extremely helpful to be able to return to a well thought out proposal to put everything back into context.

The proposal is also important for the research supervisor or manager, who has the task of ensuring that the work programme does not slip, that the emphasis remains consistent, that blind alleys are avoided and that the research staff remain highly motivated. The supervisor may also have to report on progress to other people within the organization. The proposal helps with all these things.

The proposal is crucial if, as often happens, there is a change in research staff during the course of the project. Individual research staff bring their own interpretation to their work but this should always happen within the overall intent of the project. However, when a member of the research team is replaced, the replacement may find it difficult to pick up the threads of the work and it is often necessary to go back to the proposal to put everything into context.

Towards the end of the project, the proposal helps with the interpretation of results. When researchers are faced with numerous tables on computer printout, or the accumulated results of a number of interviews, or the seemingly contradictory results of an experimental project, they frequently experience bewilderment as to the purpose of all the information. That is the time to go back to the objective and specific aims of the research and to plan the analysis and the interpretation with these in mind.

Similarly, the proposal can provide the shape for the final report and, in particular, can indicate the audience at which the report and any other dissemination activity can be directed.

All in all, the proposal provides a means of ensuring that the wood does not become obscured by the trees.

To demonstrate competence
This is the main function of a proposal for research leading to academic or professional qualifications. It is also an important factor when applying for external funding. The people to whom the proposal is directed will need to be satisfied that the

73

proposer is capable of satisfactorily undertaking and completing the work.

The proposal principally provides the applicant with a means of showing their familiarity with the subject of the research, the background context, the methods to be used and the particular relevance of other work, especially that associated with the institution to which the application is made.

If successful, the proposal will form the basis for continuing discussions with the research supervisor or the funding body. The proposal should not, however, be regarded as immutable. Changes will inevitably be called for as the work progresses and as new insights become apparent. Both parties – researcher and supervisor – should, however, beware of straying too far from the original intent of the work.

To obtain financial support for the research
It will be necessary to prepare a proposal if it is intended to seek financial support for the research. This will be the case if application is made to an external funding agency or if an application needs to be processed through the parent organization's research committee. In both these cases the proposal has to argue the case for awarding the money and show that the intending researchers are likely to make good use of the funds. In both cases it is likely that the proposal will be used to obtain expert advice from a number of referees, who will be asked to comment on the need for the research, the methods proposed and the resources required. The referees will have only the proposal to go on and it is therefore vital that it answers all the possible questions which they might raise and provides them with enough information on which to base their comments.

The first thing the proposal must do is demonstrate clearly that the proposed research falls within the terms of reference of the organization from which funds are sought. Nearly all research funders provide clear guidance on this matter and it is simply wasteful of everyone's time to produce and submit proposals to organizations that are not empowered to support in that particular area. This seems self-evident, but it is surprising how many potential researchers begin the long process of obtaining financial support by trying to persuade funding bodies to alter their terms of reference.

For an organization to commit funds to a research project, it must be convinced of the need for the research. This should come out quite clearly in the proposal. Evidence of need can come from recommendations made in previous research reports, from official reports, from the expressed views of practitioners or from the conclusions of a preliminary 'quick and dirty' study. These should be documented and cited in full. Where a document is unlikely to be easily obtainable by the funding agency it is often worth enclosing a copy. This is particularly the case with internal reports.

Closely related to the demonstration of need is the requirement to show how the proposed research fits in with other research on related topics. Most funding agencies are bureaucracies and they tend to like to see that individual research projects build on what has gone before, thus increasing the value of the previous results and possibly producing economies, in that preliminary work can be avoided if it has been covered elsewhere. There is also a tendency for funding bodies to see each project contributing to a totality of research results which will, if given enough money, solve all the problems within sight. (The totality of results, however, seldom extends beyond the projects which the agency has funded.)

Funding agencies do not wish to take undue risks with their resources, indeed in many cases the agency is charged with the responsibility of dispensing public funds. They therefore wish to see evidence that the researcher is competent to undertake the work. This means that the proposal should demonstrate familiarity with the topic, the research methods, other research and any related developments. Previous research experience is obviously relevant, as may be the positions held by the applicant.

Closely related to the funding bodies' desire to obtain value for money is the desire to ensure that the research has a degree of relevance beyond the confines of the organization within which it takes place. There must be some evidence that it will be possible to generalize from the results of the research and to apply them elsewhere. That done, it is usual to indicate that the rest of the world is, in fact, likely to be receptive to the results. If the organization applying for the research grant is the only one to have identified the problem, the take-up of results is unlikely to be great, no matter how generalizable are the results.

This leads on to dissemination. The proposal should indicate quite clearly how the results of the research are to be communicated. Just about every research project produces a report. Many go no further and the results remain entombed in a very formal, and often seldom-read, document. For every research project it is worth asking whether this is enough. There is plenty of scope for passing on the results through the publication of journal articles, the organization of seminars, workshops and conferences and by delivering papers at relevant meetings. Any plans along these lines should be set out in the proposal. It all helps to show that you are sufficiently committed to the project to want to communicate the results to others.

The funding agency will need to know exactly what its money is to be spent on, and the costings given in the proposal should be as detailed as possible. The format for setting out the costings will vary with each agency and applicants should always follow the format required. The costings should make clear whether they allow for inflation and, for example, whether the salary costs include superannuation and national insurance. Large items of expenditure should be itemized separately and an indication should be given of the likely cash flow, noting whether it is likely to be even during the course of the project, or whether there are likely to be times of a higher than average expenditure. All this will be required by the funding agency, which needs to plan its expenditure flows.

The proposal provides the basis for accountability. Sometimes it becomes part of the contract between the funding body and the researcher. As such it will be used by the funder to monitor the progress of the work and to ensure accountability for the expenditure of its funds. It is important, therefore, that the proposal contains full information about the timetable for the project, the different activities which will take place and the likely outcomes of each stage. Any major changes to these elements made during the course of the project should, of course, be notified to the funding body.

Finally, the proposal should indicate the contribution which the applicant is likely to make to the overall costs of the project. In the case of individuals, this is unlikely to be great, although even a small contribution in kind will serve as evidence of commitment. In the case of libraries or information units applying for research funds, the funding body will want some evidence that the institution does not intend to rely wholly on the external finance. It is likely that the contribution will be in kind and it is unlikely to be large, but if the institution can indicate that it is prepared to absorb the travel and subsistence costs, or the postage, stationery and telephone costs, this indicates a degree of support for and commitment to the project.

The structure of proposals
A good thing to begin with is the title. This should be sufficiently precise to indicate the nature and scope of the project but be concise enough to be referred to quickly and easily, possibly being used for specially designed headed note-paper and other stationery. It is also useful to have a short, memorable title for questionnaires and other documents issued by the project. It is usually difficult to find a title which fulfils all these requirements and the normal approach is to resort to a snappy title with an explanatory subtitle which can be included when necessary.

Let us suppose that we are preparing a proposal to seek financial support for a research project to investigate the extent to which public libraries have made use of special, external sources of finance to develop particular projects and services. An appropriate title and subtitle for the project is:

Financing development: the use of external funds by public libraries.

The first substantial section of the proposal will be the introduction to the research. This will place the work in context and set the scene for all that follows. It should be sufficiently interesting to awaken the interest of referees, research funders and anyone else likely to read the proposal. It should also be concise.

The introduction should begin by putting the research into context. It might be that the work has a particularly significant historical context, in which case this will provide the focus for the section. Otherwise the context will be provided by the need for the research and by other relevant research upon which this project will build. This section should also include the indication of the audience for the results and the likely take-up.

The introduction is also the place to show the applicant's interest in the research, familiarity with the topic and previous relevant experience. These matters will probably be covered in more detail in the section on staffing but it may be worth putting something in here, or in some other way to indicate that the applicant knows what he or she is talking about.

In our example the introduction could be covered quite concisely by the following two paragraphs:

Public libraries are making increased use of external funds to finance new developments or specific activities. These funds come from a wide variety of sources, ranging from the government, with programmes such as the Urban Programme, to the private sector, with foundations and trusts providing grants for new developments. In some cases, there has been a significant shift from recurrent funding by the local authority to *ad hoc* external funding. All the signs indicate that this trend is likely to continue. For example, in his report on library and information matters during 1984, the minister for Arts and Libraries encouraged public libraries to make use of external sources of finance 'which can enhance the available funds and so improve the quality of the service'.
(*Report by the Minister for the Arts on Library and Information Matters during 1984*, London, HMSO, 1985.)

A recent report by LAMSAC (*Income Generation in Public Libraries*, LAMSAC, 1983) explored the extent to which income can be generated through fines, fees and direct charges. This proposal is for a small study to explore the nature and extent of the use of external development funds by public libraries and to assess the impact of their use.

The scene having been set, the second section deals with the objective of the research and the specific aims. These should flow quite naturally from what has gone before and they usually require little qualification. The only qualification necessary would be, for example, if one aim was contingent upon another.

In our example, the objective and aims of the project are quite clear:

Objective
The objective of the study is to explore the nature and extent of the use of external funds by public libraries and to assess the impact of their use.

Specific aims
Within this overall objective, the study has three specific aims:

- to identify the sources of external funds available to public libraries;

- to explore the extent to which these funds have been used by public libraries;

- to explore the impact of these funds on the overall development of public library services.

The objective and aims are followed by the section on the methods used to be in the project. This is the part of the proposal which most often presents people with problems. It should not, however, be difficult if adequate prior thought and planning has taken place. Much of what follows in the proposal will depend on the methods – staff required, financial support, and so on – and if it is not possible to describe with confidence what is involved, it makes it difficult to place much credibility in the whole proposal. Assuming that the most appropriate methods have been selected, they will need to be described in such a way that it is obvious how they will be used. This section will be referred to by the research staff seeking guidance, by the project supervisor or manager and by any external funder and it must meet all of their needs.

The research staff will want to find guidance about how individual methods are to be applied to the specific problems of this particular project. They will want to know, for example, how questionnaires are to be distributed, whether they are going to be supplemented by in-depth interviews, and so on. The project supervisor will need to be able to see how the different methods complement each other and how they contribute to the overall results. The supervisor will also need to know what difficult areas are likely to be encountered. The funding agency will need to see that the applicant is sufficiently familiar with the methods to avoid the problems associated with them.

The art lies in reconciling all these different needs and in writing something which provides sufficient information while allowing for the fact that modifications will inevitably be required once the project gets going.

Do not forget that dissemination is part of the research methodology and should be covered in this section.

For our project it is possible to use the three specific aims to provide the structure for the section on methods to be used. A combination of desk research, postal questionnaires and in-depth interviews will be used to collect the information for the research and it is necessary to show how these will complement each other.

The sources of external funds

This part of the study would aim to identify the various sources of funds and, wherever possible, to specify the purpose, accessibility and particular terms of reference associated with the funds. The information would be gathered by desk research and correspondence with the funding agencies. Where necessary, direct personal contact will be made with the funding bodies. The information gathered in this part of the study would be presented in the report, in the form of a directory.

The extent of use

To compile a full picture of the extent of use, it will be necessary to undertake a survey of all public library authorities in the United Kingdom. The survey would be kept as simple as possible and would involve a postal questionnaire sent to each chief librarian. Information would be sought about the projects which had been funded from external sources during the previous financial year. In addition less detailed information would be sought on the situation in the preceding four years.

Care would be taken to pilot the questionnaire so as to ensure that it did not place unreasonable burdens on the librarians. The data collected would be processed manually.

The impact on the service
To obtain a thorough view of the impact which external funds have on public library services it will be necessary to carry out in-depth interviews with a number of public librarians. The aim here will be to collect information about the purposes to which the funds have been put, their long-term effect, the impact on the rest of the service, the influence on innovation, the extent to which priorities become distorted by the availability of external funds, and the likely future position.

The results of the questionnaire survey will provide the basis for selecting the authorities within which such interviews will take place.

Dissemination
One concrete product of the study would be a directory of external sources of funds. At present, the intention is to publish this directory as part of the final report on the project. It would, however, be possible to publish it as a separate volume. The research report would also analyse the extent and impact of use.

If necessary, the report and the directory could be launched at a workshop for public librarians.

The section on methods is usually followed by a section on the staffing of the project. There are basically three types of staff associated with any research project – the researchers themselves, the research supervisor and the support staff.

The section on staffing will depend very much on whether you are specifying the skills and experience which you will seek when recruiting someone to the research position or whether you are describing the particular skills and abilities of the staff who you know will be undertaking the work.

The researchers will form the bulk of the staff. Careful thought needs to be given to the skills and experience required for the work. The choice may be limited, in which case it is still worth giving the matter some thought as it might be possible to overcome deficiencies in another way, by involving a consultant. If the staff are to be recruited specifically for the project, their requirements should be made clear in the proposal. It would not be unreasonable to expect some research experience and a degree of familiarity with the research methods which will be used. It should be remembered that, because research does not provide steady employment, it is usually necessary to pay a slightly higher salary than would be usual for a permanent post at that level.

The research supervisor plays a vital role in a research project and has the task of remaining sufficiently detached to be able to steer the course of the work without becoming bogged down in the detail. Yet the supervisor must be sufficiently familiar with the subject and the progress of the research to be able to take part in discussions about future lines of development or the significance of unexpected findings. The applicant will frequently be in the position of supervising the research, in which case the proposal should indicate his or her suitability for the task. The supervisor is sometimes assisted by a steering or advisory committee and if so, the proposal should indicate it, giving a list of the likely members of the committee.

The support staff can also play an important part in making a success of the research. The clerical staff will work closely with the researchers and should be chosen so as to avoid any personality clashes. It may be necessary to allow for additional assistance at certain periods during the research. Other support staff who might be required are computing staff, interviewers and other fieldworkers. In some cases, provision is made for the employment of a consultant to provide specialist advice and assistance. Again, this should be indicated and it is usual to name the consultant proposed.

Finally, this section should indicate whether staff are to be recruited to the project, whether they are to be released on secondment or whether they are already employed.

In our example, the work will be carried out by two people who are already employed as researchers and the section on staffing, therefore, is primarily concerned to demonstrate their competence for the task. In this particular project, supervision would be provided by a small advisory committee of public librarians. The section in the proposal is as follows:

Staffing
The research will be carried out by John Smith and Susan Jones. Both are permanently employed as Senior Research Workers.

John Smith has a background in public librarianship and considerable experience of conducting research and investigations into the management and financing of public libraries.

Susan Jones has experience of research in local government and, in particular, considerable experience with in-depth interviewing.

Supervision of the project would be provided by a small Advisory Committee consisting of no more than three chief public librarians and, if thought desirable, a representative of the funding body. It is envisaged that the Advisory Committee will meet no more than three times during the course of the project. Meetings will be convened and administered by the research team.

Clerical support will be provided from the resources of the research organization.

After staffing, come the details of the timing of the project. Unless the work is to be tied in to specific periods in the year, it is usual, when applying to funding agencies, to express the timetable in weeks, beginning at week one and working on from there. This avoids any problems which might arise from the funding agency's inability to produce the money by a specified date.

This section should make clear the overall duration of the project, the amount of time each of the main tasks will require and the sequence in which they will occur. It is important to differentiate between the time required for a researcher to carry out a task and the elapsed time which will be required, allowing for unproductive periods.

It is usual to provide some form of chart, indicating the pattern of work and the sequence of activities. This will prove invaluable as a means of checking progress and ensuring that the timetable is adhered to.

Finally, it is necessary to allow for holidays and periods of sickness. It is also sensible to build into the timetable an allowance for slippage in the work, although with well-run projects this should not be necessary. It is also worth remembering that funding bodies usually look askance at proposals that include three months at the end of the research for writing up the report.

The calculation of timing and duration for our project is relatively straightforward. Even here, however, it is necessary to think through the sequence of events. For example, when carrying out the in-depth interviews with the chief librarians, the researchers should be more than just familiar with the sources of funds available. So the interviews must follow the desk research. It is also necessary to remember that the administration of the postal questionnaire will take a long time from the initial design to the receipt of all the responses. Further, it will not be possible to select the authorities for interview until a substantial number of questionnaires has been returned. It will, however, be possible to design and to pilot the interview schedule. Finally, to avoid the need to process all the data at the end of the project, it is always worth planning to start the analysis about half way through so that data can be processed when it is being collected and assembled ready for incorporation in the final report. As to the actual number of days work required, this can only really be estimated on the basis of experience and a detailed understanding of the speed at which the research workers can operate. A project such as ours could be accomplished by two experienced researchers in a total of 60 person-days, spread over a four-month period. In view of this, the section on timing and duration in the proposal would appear something like this:

Timing and duration

The time required for the different stages of the project is as follows:

- the source of external funds   10 person-days
- the extent of use   25 person-days
- the impact of the service   15 person-days
- analysis and report production   10 person-days

The work will be carried out in the sequence shown in Table 1.

The project will, therefore, require 60 person-days spread over a total elapsed time of four months.

TABLE 1. Financing development: sequence of work

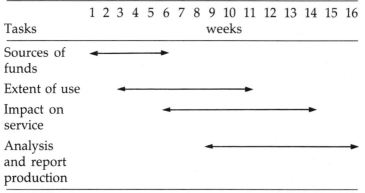

Tasks	1 2 3 4 5 6 7 8 9 10 11 12 13 14 15 16 weeks
Sources of funds	
Extent of use	
Impact on service	
Analysis and report production	

The costing is an essential element of a proposal. Even if external funding is not sought, it is worth calculating the cost of the work, if only to be sure that the results are likely to justify the expenditure. If preparing a costing for an application for external finance, there are some elementary rules to follow. First of all, find out what costing conventions the funding agency uses and follow them. In particular, set out the different items of expenditure in the format required. Give a clear indication of whether allowance has been made for inflation and, in the case of salaries, whether allowance has been made for superannuation and national insurance. For items such as travel and subsistence, it is normal to follow the practice of the host institution, unless the funding agency has its own arrangements.

If the funding body does not provide any guidance on costing it is possible to set out the information in a fairly standard way which should meet all the requirements. The costs are broken down into staff costs, travel and subsistence, recurrent costs and non-recurrent costs.

Staff costs include the salaries, superannuation and national insurance of all staff employed on the project. It is usual to pay staff on salary scales recognized by the host institution, and in the proposal it is customary to give the scale, the range and the incremental point at which an appointment is likely to be made. For projects lasting more than a year, allowance should be made for annual increments.

Increasingly, it is common to express the staff costs in terms of rate per day worked. When calculating this rate, it is not sufficient simply to divide an annual salary by 365. Allowance needs to be made for public holidays, weekends, annual leave, periods of sickness, as well as the often overlooked fact that each project carries with it a considerable amount of time spent in negotiation at the beginning and in disseminating at the end. As a general rule of thumb, work on the basis that people employed on a daily rate can seldom manage to fit in more than 100–120 paid days work each year. It may also be necessary to allow for superannuation and national insurance.

Travel and subsistence costs are self explanatory, although it is important to be clear about any inflation allowances and to indicate whether there will be any periods during the project when expenditure under this heading will be particularly high.

Recurrent costs cover postage, stationery, telephone, printing, computer charges and any other items of expenditure which will recur during the course of the project. Non-recurrent costs are those one-off items which do not recur. If a seminar was costed into the project it would be allowed for under this heading, as would any equipment required. It is usual to itemize any expenditure under this heading. The only other point to remember is to indicate, for projects lasting more than one year, how much will be required during each financial year. This information will be required by the funding agency for its planning.

The costing for our project is quite straightforward. The staff cost is calculated on a rate per day and the only other costs are those associated with travel and subsistence and the recurrent costs of typing, photocopying and so on. The costing section in the report, therefore appears like this:

Costing	£
• Staff cost	
– 60 days at £100 per day	6000.00
• Travel and subsistence	
– various journeys within the UK	550.00
• Recurrent costs	
– typing, photocopying, telephone,	
stationery, printing, etc.	500.00
Total	£7050.00

The work and consequently all the payments will fall in the current financial year.

The final point to note about the proposal, particularly if it is being used to obtain financial support from an outside organization, is that it should look good. A well laid out proposal, which looks as if it has been carefully considered, creates a much better initial impression with funders, referees and research staff than one that looks as if it has been thrown together that morning on the way to work. Remember that the proposal will quite likely be used to sell the research and the researchers and it should, therefore, look as professional as possible. When put together, the proposal for our project looks like this.

**Financing development:
the use of external funds by public libraries**

A proposal submitted by Research Associates

Public libraries are making increased use of external funds to finance new developments or specific activities. These funds come from a wide variety of sources, ranging from

---

the government, with programmes such as the Urban Programme, to the private sector, with foundations and trusts providing grants for new developments. In some cases there has been a significant shift from recurrent funding by local authority to *ad hoc* external funding. All the signs indicate that this trend is likely to continue. For example, in his report on library and information matters during 1984, the Minister for Arts and Libraries encouraged public libraries to make use of external sources of finance 'which can enhance the available funds and so improve the quality of the service'. (*Report by the Minister for the Arts on Library and Information Matters during 1984*, London, HMSO, 1985.)

A recent report by LAMSAC (*Income Generation in Public Libraries*, LAMSAC, 1983) explored the extent to which income can be generaged through fines, fees and direct charges. This proposal is for a small study to explore the nature and extent of the use of external development funds by public libraries and to assess the impact of their use.

Objective
The objective of the study is to explore the nature and extent of the use of external funds by public libraries and to assess the impact of their use.

Specific aims
Within this overall objective the study has three specific aims:

- to identify the sources of external funds available to public libraries;

- to explore the extent to which these funds have been used by public libraries;

- to explore the impact of these funds on the development of public library services.

88

The sources of external funds
This part of the study would aim to identify the various sources of funds and, wherever possible, to specify the purpose, accessibility and particular terms of reference associated with the funds. The information would be gathered by a process of desk research and correspondence with the funding agencies. Where necessary, direct personal contact will be made with the funding bodies. The information gathered in this part of the study would be presented in the report in the form of a directory.

The extent of use
To compile a full picture of the extent of use, it will be necessary to undertake a survey of all public library authorities in the United Kingdom. The survey would be kept as simple as possible and would involve a postal questionnaire sent to each chief librarian. Information would be sought about the projects which had been funded from external sources during the previous financial year. Less detailed information would be sought on the situation in the preceding four years.

Care would be taken to pilot the questionnaire so as to ensure that it did not place unreasonable burdens on the librarians. The data collected would be processed manually.

The impact on the service
To obtain a thorough view of the impact which external funds have on public library services it will be necessary to carry out in-depth interviews with a number of public librarians. The aim here will be to collect information about the purposes to which the funds have been put, their long-term effect, the impact on the rest of the service, the influence on innovation, the extent to which priorities become distorted by the availability of external funds, and the likely future position.

The results of the questionnaire survey will provide the basis for selecting the authorities within which such interviews will take place.

Dissemination

One concrete product of the study would be a directory of external sources of funds. At present, the intention is to publish this directory as part of the final report on the project. It would, however, be possible to publish it as a separate volume. The research report would also analyse the extent and impact of use.

If necessary, the report and the directory could be launched at a workshop for public librarians.

Staffing

The research would be carried out by John Smith and Susan Jones. Both are permanently employed as Senior Research Workers.

John Smith has a background in public librarianship and considerable experience of conducting research and investigations into the management and financing of public libraries.

Susan Jones has experience of research in local government and, in particular, considerable experience with in-depth interviewing.

Supervision of the project would be provided by a small Advisory Committee consisting of no more than three chief public librarians and, if thought desirable, a representative of the funding body. It is envisaged that the Advisory Committee will meet no more than three times during the course of the project. Meetings will be convened and administered by the research team.

Clerical support will be provided from the resources of the research questionnaire.

Timing and duration

The time required for the different stages of the project is as follows:

- the source of external funds   10 person-days
- the extent of use   25 person-days
- the impact of the service   15 person-days
- analysis and report production   10 person-days

The work would be carried out in the sequence shown in Table 1.

The project would, therefore, require 60 person-days spread over a total elapsed time of four months.

Costing	£
• Staff cost	
– 60 days at £100 per day	6000.00
• Travel and subsistence	
– various journeys within the UK	550.00
• Recurrent costs	
– typing, photocopying, telephone, stationery, printing, etc.	500.00
Total	£7050.00

The work and consequently all the payments will fall in the current financial year.

The actual form of the proposal and the detail contained in it will obviously vary from project to project. The proposal used as an example for this chapter was in fact based on a real research project which was funded by the British Library Research and Development Department (Nick Moore and Elaine Kempson, *Financing development: the use of external funds by public libraries*, Bath, Parker Moore Ltd, 1986; available from Parker Moore Ltd, 10 Circus Mews, Bath BA1 2PW.)

4

Obtain financial support

Research can be expensive. Fortunately, increasing number of organizations accept the expense as a necessary part of maintaining the efficiency of the organization and its responsiveness to the needs of its users. Consequently, many research projects are funded from the resources of the organizations in which they are based. It is, however, sometimes necessary to look for external sources of funds. It may be that the project simply is beyond the scope of the available resources, or that it is felt to have a wider relevance, which would justify external support. In other instances, individuals seek research funds to allow them to develop a particular interest or to undertake research leading to an academic or professional qualification.

All of these cases will involve the submission of an application to a source of funds, a process of negotiation and approval or rejection. For those who succeed, there then begins the often troublesome experience of 'living with your funder'.

Is it really worth it?
This question is often asked by applicants who have spent a long time preparing submissions, revising them, negotiating, renegotiating and resubmitting, only to be told that this year's funds have all been allocated, but there is just a chance that next year . . . It is a question worth asking well before that stage is reached.

'Is it really worth it?'

Research grants are time-consuming to obtain, as anyone who has tried it will agree. There is also considerable competition for a limited supply of funds. The procedures adopted by the funding agencies differ, and to become fully conversant with even one can be a lengthy process. It is obviously not worth going to all the trouble unless the grant is going to be large enough to make it all worthwhile. That being said, funding bodies often have separate funds allocated for small projects which require a less formal application, and these are often well worth exploring.

The very fact that research takes place with external finance places constraints on the project. The funding bodies will probably have their own specific requirements which must be met. Few of them now require formal interim reports during the project, but they all have informal conditions. They may want specific areas highlighted, or the researchers to look in particular at an aspect which was not central to the original design. They frequently insist on steering committees or advisory committees which have to be serviced and fed with information if they are to operate successfully. The very existence of the grant can induce an element of caution and can lead to a tendency to present results in such a way as not to offend the funder, or to emphasize aspects of the problem in which the funding body is known to have an interest.

On the other hand, the existence of the research grant can enhance a project. Simply by making available the resources required to do the job properly the grant can make the difference between a satisfactory project and one which fails for lack of time or the ability to cover sufficient ground.

Obtaining a grant also gives the project a seal of approval, and can provide access to all sorts of help which might not otherwise be forthcoming. Indeed, this is often arranged by the funding body, which might suggest the use of a consultant or put the researchers in touch with others who have tackled similar problems. It is also a means of getting into the network of researchers which tends to focus on a particular funding agency. The knowledge that an external organization is funding the research can do much to provide the necessary discipline required if the work is to cover all the ground and remain on schedule.

Finally, the grant and the publicity associated with its award help to create an awareness of the existence of the work. Researchers often avoid publicity, usually not wishing to appear unduly keen to attract personal attention. It is, however, important that other people know about the research. If the existence of the project is known, other researchers and interested practitioners will tend to come forward with useful information, contacts are made which later in the project can provide an opportunity to discuss problems and difficulties, and, most of all, disseminating the results of the work can begin from the word go.

Choose the source of finance

Research funds are available from a wide variety of sources, all of which should be considered at the beginning. The first one to look at is the parent organization itself. Within the local authority, academic institution, company or corporation there may be a research fund which could provide all the resources required. Little is usually known about these funds and it often requires some detective work to discover that they exist and how access to them may be gained. The best places to begin looking are research departments, chief executive's departments and anything with the words 'corporate', 'planning' or 'studies' in the title.

Outside the immediate organization the choice is wide. The field is dominated by funding agencies such as research councils and other public bodies which have the award of research grants as one of their specific functions. Government departments often come into this category. Outside the public sector are the charitable foundations and trusts. These vary from the very large organizations which dispense many thousands of pounds each year to the smaller trusts which may have only a small sum of money at their disposal. It is obviously important to find out at an early stage whether the scale of operation is likely to suit the grant for which you are applying.

Professional associations often have small research funds, although these are sadly vulnerable in times of financial pressure. Even if a professional association does not have a specific research fund it may be responsible for organizing competitions and regular awards in the form of bursaries and scholarships which can be used for research purposes. Such competitions are sometimes arranged by commercial suppliers or publishers specializing in the field.

Commercial sponsorship is becoming more common these days. This is when a commercial firm is asked to contribute towards the cost of a specific project. This is possibly the most uncertain of the sources of dunds, as much depends on the organization, the relevance of the research and the current level of profits, but it is worth considering even though the demand for funds usually greatly exceeds the supply.

The other form of funding which is growing in importance is consortium funding. Again, this is not a well-established route to funds and much depends on the particular circumstances. The idea is to get several organizations that would benefit from the research to contribute a small amount of money each, and in this way build up a fund to finance the research. Research funds built up like this demonstrate the commitment of the organizations concerned and can often attract a matching grant from a government department.

Once all the possibilities have been considered, it should be possible to select the type of funding body which is most likely to be interested in funding the research. It is worth making the selection quite specific at this stage as it can considerably reduce the time spent trying to interest people in the project. It is, after all, always possible to spread the net a little wider after an initial approach to the three or four most likely sources.

Having selected the type of funding agency, the next step is to track down all the possibilities within the type and obtain all the relevant literature, guides and application forms. The first things to look for in this information are the terms of reference of the agency. This will usually be a fairly precise statement which provides the boundaries within which the agency is prepared to consider applications. There may be a set of terms of reference which remain unchanged – this is usually the case with old established trusts, or the agency may announce that, within an overall set of terms, it is proposing to concentrate on specific aspects and, by implication, is not interested in anything else. Alternatively, the terms of reference will be changed and modified to meet different circumstances, in which case the only safe way to proceed is to ring up and try to sell the idea to the agency.

It is possible to short-cut much of this work by discussing sources of finance with other researchers. They will have had experience of some of the agencies and can advise which are to be avoided. Another approach is to contact one of the agencies which seems helpful but has terms of reference which do not really extend to the research project in hand. If the agency is doing its job properly, it will refer any such applicants to the agency which is most likely to consider funding a project on that topic. Official public bodies and large foundations are usually best at this.

It should now be possible to refine the list of possibles down to one obvious contender plus a couple of reserves. At this stage, it is necessary to look in detail at the guides to applicants, general information and anything else it is possible to extract from them. Things to look out for are: the existence of any deadlines for submission of applications; the nature, and in particular, the likely size of the application and supporting proposal; the arrangements for refereeing and approval of the award; and any conditions placed on the grant, for example, many charitable trusts are empowered to award grants only to registered charities.

All this information takes time to gather and to digest. Most of it, however, is relevant for each application, so the burden reduces as time goes on. This does mean, however, that academics and professional researchers are usually in a better position to obtain grants than is the practitioner undertaking the task for the first time.

Make the approach

Before starting any negotiations with a funding body it is always advisable to try to think of things from their position. The people with whom the discussions will take place will be interested in the subject of the research, but they are unlikely to have had any recent direct experience of the problems faced by the applicant. They will be concerned about allocating limited resources between a number of competing applications. They will also be worried about actually spending their allocation of money during the financial year and will attempt to avoid both under- and over-spending. Subject to these overriding constraints, they will be looking for interesting and novel projects which are felt to be relevant to expressed needs and which are likely to be carried out in a competent and professional manner. The projects should have a high expectation of producing good, interesting reports, which will make an impact on those concerned with the subject. There is usually a tendency to avoid the contentious and the controversial, although, equally, there will be little support for very bland research projects which are unlikely to cause any ripples at all.

Inevitably, the funding body will have its own set of rules and precedents which will govern the award of the grant. These should be discovered as soon as possible and every step should be taken to ensure that the project meets all of the criteria adopted.

Bearing these points in mind, the prospective researcher should make a first informal approach to the funder. The task at this stage is to interest the funder in the idea, establish that it falls within the terms of reference and meets all the selection criteria, or could be modified or strengthened to do so. The essence of the project should be set down on a single sheet of paper at this stage, and this should form the basis for the initial discussions. With luck the funder will offer advice on how the proposal should be drafted. This will include indications of points which need emphasis, any additions needed and any aspects which should be played down. It is usual to make a formal application using the funder's own forms and to support this with a proposal. The exact style will need to be discussed with the funder.

Now is also the time to ask whether the grant includes items such as dissemination activities, administrative overheads, salary costs of the supervisor and so on. Other matters which could be discussed, if they are not obvious from the available literature, are whether there are likely to be any hold-ups with the payment of the money; how and when claims should be submitted; whether an advisory committee will be required; how the proposal will be refereed; and whether there are any deadlines for the submission of the application.

Assuming that the response to this initial approach is favourable, the next stage is to act on the advice given and to produce a full proposal to support the formal application. This should not take long as all the basic preparation should have been done and it should simply be a matter of re-drafting the proposal into the required format. It obviously creates a good impression if the required proposal is submitted as soon as possible after the initial interview. It is worth reinforcing this by ensuring that the proposal looks professional, is well set out and is devoid of typing errors. A badly proof-read proposal does not encourage confidence in a researcher's ability to undertake careful analysis of complex data.

Now begins the long wait. Once the full proposal has been received there can be a delay of as much as three months while it passes through the internal processes of the agency, is distributed to referees whose comments then have to be assessed, is put before one or more committees for decision, and then is ratified by the Archangel Gabriel. When the decision is announced, be prepared to make some amendments which might have been suggested by the referees, but equally be sure about those parts of the proposal which are not amenable to alteration.

If the decision is negative it is always worth exploring whether it would be possible to revise the proposal and re-submit. Alternatively there might be other ways in which the application could be made acceptable. Having got this far it is worth exploring all the possibilities. If it still proves unsuccessful, take a close look at the proposal and the project, perhaps sending it to a researcher whose views can be trusted and ask for an honest evaluation. If the project still apears viable, move on to one of the reserves and begin the process again.

Living with the funder

Once the grant is awarded, the funder's interest focuses on three things: a successful project which will do credit to the organization; spending the budgeted amount of money, no more and no less; and a good report showing that the work was carried out successfully. It is possible to begin a successful relationship with the funding body by working towards a project which will meet its research objectives and those of the funder. Begin by getting the project going on time. Allow sufficient time for appointing staff, occupying office accommodation and so on.

After the project has been going a couple of months, invite the relevant person in the funding body to visit the project to see how things are going.

Having started the relationship well, build on it by keeping the funder well informed about progress, sending in any reports produced, discussion papers and other significant documents. If there is an advisory committee, make good use of it. A good advisory committee can be of great help to a project, but, again, the researcher needs to work at it. The members of the advisory committee need to feel that they have a significant job to do. This means keeping them informed about progress, not simply sending a great wad of papers for them to look at on the way to the meeting. It also means asking them for advice on important points, and being ready to act upon the advice given. A golden rule with Advisory Committees is that if there are any points on which you do not want advice, do not ask for it. If possible, ensure that the funding body is represented on the advisory committee.

Problems will inevitably arise during the project, and sometimes these will involve matters which are the concern of the funder. Always ensure that the funder is informed about these as soon as they arise. This particularly applies to unexpected fluctuations in expenditure. It is usually possible to accommodate most situations if they are tackled early enough.

As the research nears completion, discuss the main conclusions and recommendations with the funder. It should not be necessary to point out that the conclusions and recommendations are those of the project and not up for negotiation, although if this does prove to be necessary it is worth getting the battle out of the way as early as possible. Be prepared to take advice, especially over the framing of recommendations – the funder will probably have some experience of the best way of putting things so as to ensure that some action is taken on them.

Also discuss the format of the report, noting any particular requirements which they may have. Decide who is going to publish the report. Often the funding body has its own reports series but it is sometimes possible to make alternative publication arrangements. Other forms of dissemination should also be discussed, including seminars, conferences and workshops.

The final thing which will determine the quality of the relationship between funder and researcher is the latter's ability to submit the completed report on time. Few things are more calculated to reduce the chances of further grants than delays at this stage. But before thoughts move on to the next grant, stop awhile and ask that question again – 'Is it really worth it?'

5

Get the project on the road and keep it going

Successful research projects are the ones which start out well organized and continue in the same way. Much of the responsibility for this rests on the project supervisor. This is usually the person who had the idea in the first place and did all the preparatory work involved with selecting the methods, preparing the proposal and securing the finance. It is usual for that person to take overall responsibility for the intellectual direction and the practical management of the project. With some projects, research staff are employed specifically for the project and will report to the supervisor. More usually the person who develops the research idea is the one who does most of the work, no additional staff being appointed, in which case it is advisable to have someone to take charge of administrative matters and remain sufficiently involved in the work of the project to provide a sounding board for ideas. No matter how the work is allocated, someone must agree to organize the project. This involves a fair amount of work setting things up, after which it becomes a matter of keeping things ticking over.

Staffing
The first consideration is getting the right staff appointed. The nature of the project determines the options available. For a large-scale, externally-funded project the main choice is between employing staff specifically for the project or recruiting

them from another part of the organization, to carry out the work on secondment. With smaller projects the staff are probably already allocated or, indeed, the work is carried out by the originator of the idea.

If possible it is well worth considering the idea of secondment. The advantages of it as a method of staffing research projects are that it provides staff with some continuity of employment and thus makes a research job attractive to staff who would otherwise reject a short-term contract with no prospects of further work at the end. It can also provide a form of training for operational staff and is often thought of as part of a form of staff development. From the point of view of the research it means that it is possible to have a researcher who has a close working knowledge of the system in which the research takes place, although this can have its drawbacks, as the arrangement does not enable fresh approaches to problems which might otherwise be generated by someone new to the organization.

Where staff are recruited specifically for the research project it is necessary to make the appointment in much the same way as for permanent staff, involving the personnel section, informing the trade union, drafting and placing an advertisement, drafting a job description, drawing up short-lists and interviewing. Funding bodies vary about the amount of involvement they require at this stage. Some want to approve the advertisement, comment on the short-list and be present at the interview, others let the organization get on with it.

Before interviewing, try to be sure what it is that the project requires. The choice is usually between those who have plenty of research experience but little recent practical knowledge, or those who have worked in the field but have little research knowledge. Occasionally the two attributes are combined, and these usually make the best researchers, but these are few and far between and it is normally necessary to accept a compromise candidate. Other attributes might be necessary for the job – it would be unwise, for example, to appoint a shy person to a job involving a lot of interviewing; equally, a lively extrovert might feel constrained by work involving a great deal of detailed analysis of data.

It is sometimes worth waiting until the research staff are in post before advertising for and appointing clerical staff. Not only does this increase the chance of finding someone who will work well with the researcher, but it also fits in with the pattern of work, as not much clerical work is generated in the first few weeks of the project. The supervisor should also note whether fieldwork staff are going to be required during the project and make sure that they are recruited at the right time.

An alternative way of staffing research projects is to put the work out to research consultants. The procedure for doing this varies considerably from project to project. With small projects it may simply be a case of contacting a research consultant, explaining what is needed and requesting a proposal explaining what is to be done. For bigger projects, however, it may be necessary to draw up a specification and send this out to a number of consultants, asking them to submit tenders. This approach however, goes rather beyond the scope of this book.

Finance

Even if the project is funded from within the resources of the institution, it may be necessary to make special arrangements for financial matters. It may simply be a case of getting a code number on the finance department's computer, but until that is done lots of other things can be held up.

Where external finance is involved the problems are rather more significant. Basically, it is a question of reconciling two different accounting systems. The host organization will have its own arrangements while the funding body will need to have claims presented in a form which suits its own accounting system. In between is the research project. The establishment of a good working relationship with the finance department is a high priority at this stage.

Two points in particular need to be made clear from the start – the arrangements for claiming the grant and the records of expenditure. Exactly who does what can be rather important here.

If you are in charge of the research project make sure that you receive sufficient information about expenditure on the project as it develops. In that way it may be possible to avoid the embarrassing situation of running out of money before the work is completed.

Accommodation and services

Too many researchers have arrived only to find that it has not been decided where they are to sit. Provision needs to be made for an office and access to all the usual facilities, such as telephones and photocopiers. Any equipment required should be obtained as early as possible to avoid any unnecessary delays. Major purchases of equipment might require the prior approval of the funding agency which will probably claim ownership of the item at the end of the project.

There should be an ample supply of stationery. In projects which involve a lot of correspondence, or where it is important to create a particular impression, it is worth going to the trouble of printing some headed notepaper. Alternatively, it is always possible to overprint the organization's own stationery.

Support services can be vital during the project, and those in charge of them should be given prior warning of the research. For example, if questionnaires need to be printed, it makes sense to warn the printing section so that they can programme the work into their schedule. Similarly the computing section needs to be given plenty of notice if results are to be processed by them. All these things can be sorted out easily early on. It is when they are left to the last minute that problems arise.

The problems usually arise because it is necessary to deal with people who are permanently employed and who frequently do not fully appreciate the constraints imposed by working on a project with a fixed deadline. Delays at the beginning of the project can become critical later on.

Advisory committee

The point was made in the previous chapter that these committees can prove useful if operated in the right way. This needs to start with their very selection. Advisory committee members can be selected for a number of reasons – because they bring specialized knowledge; because they represent organizations which have a particular stake in the research; or because they will help to disseminate the results of the research. On occasion, advisory committee members have been selected because they can be relied upon not to ask awkward questions or because they asked the supervisor to sit on their advisory committee last time round.

The objective when selecting the committee members must be to have people who can make a contribution. They should be able to provide assistance with the overall direction of the project and be able to offer detailed advice on specific issues. It may be uncomfortable at the time, but it is always useful to have at least one person who can be guaranteed to ask the awkward question which everyone else is studiously avoiding. If it is not asked now, it certainly will be when the report is published.

In the invitation to sit on an advisory committee there should be enough information to allow the prospective members to make up their own minds about whether they will be able to make a useful contribution. The letter should also make quite clear who will be meeting the expenses associated with attendance at the meetings, the number of meetings involved and whether the person is being invited in a personal capacity or as a representative of an organization, in which case it is usually acceptable to send a substitute. Each member should receive a copy of the proposal, the job description of the researcher and any other relevant documentation.

It is always worth deciding in advance who is to be invited to chair the meeting. If nothing else, this avoids much embarrassment at the first meeting, when it is unrealistic to ask a group of people who may not have met each other before to elect one of their number to the chair.

Other activities

An important job of the supervisor is to ensure effective communication about the project. The supervisor needs to communicate with a variety of people and organizations, and the communication needs to vary to suit the recipient. An early priority with any project taking place within an organization must be to communicate information about the research to other people in the organization. This helps to ensure co-operation in any later survey work and should help to dispel people's suspicion of research and researchers.

A good communication system needs to be established with the funder and much of this was discussed in the previous chapter. Similarly important is communication with other researchers and interested parties. Not only does this begin the process of dissemination but it also serves to attract useful information and comment from a variety of sources. Steps should be taken to announce the research in research registers and the professional press. It is also possible to use the local press to inform people of the existence of the project and generally to create an awareness of what is going on. As a result of this, the project will probably receive requests for further information, and it is often worth preparing an information sheet which can be sent out on demand.

In good research projects the process of dissemination begins when the project starts. It is not just tacked on at the end.

The other main task of the supervisor is to ensure that the project keeps to its timetable. At any given time it should be possible to say what has been done and to compare this with what should have been done by then. It is very easy for research projects to fall behind schedule, and it is incredibly difficult to make up lost time. The consequence is that all the work towards the end of the project tends to become sandwiched. The funder starts putting on pressure for the final report, and parts of the analysis have to be skimped because of the pressure of time. Often the project will end, the researchers depart and the supervisor will be left with the remains of the analysis and the report to write. Not a happy state.

It is worth having regular meetings to review progress and to take any necessary steps to avoid a bottleneck just when results need to be looked at, considered and thought about in tranquility. If the project has an advisory committee it is worth linking these progress meetings to the advisory committee meetings. But do not expect the committee to review progress – that is a job for the supervisor and research staff.

Allied to the progress of the work is the progress of the expenditure. Claims should be submitted regularly and on time. It is normal practice to claim research grants quarterly in arrears

'Getting started can be the most difficult part . . .'

and it will help the funding body if these claims are submitted promptly, particularly at the end of the financial year.

At the end of the project the supervisor will have to consider dissemination arrangements in general and the report in particular. It obviously makes sense to complete the report when the researchers and clerical staff are still around. If it is not done then it can become an intolerable burden which can hang around for months, souring the carefully nurtured relationship with the funder. All the necessary arrangements should be made to type and print the required number of copies in the format specified by the funder. Once this has been done and any arrangements made for further dissemination, the supervisor can relax and begin to think about the next project.

So far, we have been mainly concerned with the functions of the supervisor. We can now turn to the job of the actual researcher. In many cases the two jobs will be carried out by the same person. In others the research work will be undertaken by the person who generated the ideas in the first place and who did all the basic thinking necessary to formulate the proposal and set up the project. In the remainder of cases the researcher will be employed to work on a project which has been developed by the supervisor, and the researcher will thus come without much prior knowledge of the detail and development of the project. These different relationships between the researcher and the project obviously condition the way in which the work is approached, but once the researcher has started the differences diminish.

The research approach adopted by the project and the methods used will also determine the work that actually takes place. There are, however, some general principles and guidelines which apply to all projects. What follows is an attempt to bring together all the lessons that might benefit anyone embarking on the actual business of research.

Getting started

Getting started can be the most difficult part, particularly if the researcher is coming to the project for the first time. In such cases the first priority is to understand what the project is all about. The starting point for this is the proposal but it is

'. . . ensure that the project keeps to its timetable.'

necessary to go beyond this and to look at the factors which influenced the first ideas about the work and how the situation has developed since that time. It is often helpful to look at early drafts of the proposal to see how that developed, particularly if major changes were made at the request of a funding agency. The project supervisor will be the most obvious source of information at this stage, and it is important to begin what is an important relationship by making sure that both parties understand each other and the reason which took them to their current positions. Look for the underlying motives and hidden agendas.

As well as understanding the background to the project, it is necessary to build up an understanding of the project or area in which the research is taking place. Even researchers who have been responsible for developing the ideas may find it useful to try to approach the subject afresh, perhaps consulting material which might previously have been passed over.

There will not be sufficient time to begin a major study of the background subject, involving much reading of the standard works. Far better to concentrate on the more popular material, especially periodicals. These give a clearer impression of the important issues and will rapidly build up the sort of familiarity with places, personalities and jargon which will be necessary when relating to practitioners in the field.

It is equally important to develop familiarity with the research methods to be used in the project. A limited amount can be picked up from books about research methodology, but there is no substitute for talking to people who have actually used different methods and who are likely to be aware of the limitations and tricks of the trade. It is worth trying to get hold of some research reports on projects that used the same methods, to build up a picture of how they can be applied, the type of questionnaires used and so on.

The next stage is to establish a timetable or work schedule. This must be realistic and sufficiently honest to give concern if the work begins to fall behind schedule. It is advisable to build in a certain amount of slippage to allow for unforeseen circumstances, and allow six to eight weeks for each person, each year, for holidays and sickness.

It is as well to begin the project by being well organized. Have the research office as you want it, remembering, where appropriate, to allow plenty of space for large numbers of survey forms and sufficient room to spread things out when analysing the information. Start a card file of useful names and addresses. It can be invaluable not only during the course of the work but also when it comes to disseminating the results. In carrying out all this work, the aim should be to build up a momentum which will carry through the whole project.

Keeping going

The first thing to become apparent is the time constraint under which the work takes place. It is essential not to get behind schedule and one implication of this is that it is seldom possible to repeat something or to have another go at something that did not seem right the first time. (The only exceptions to this are questionnaires and interview schedules.) It is worth aiming to get everything right first time.

If the work does slip behind schedule, to an extent that causes concern, even allowing for the slippage built into the timetable, do not ignore it. It is sensible to review the position and to see what can be cut out or reduced in scale. Far better to do this at an early stage. The alternative is to find that everything needs to be hurried during the closing stages of the project and the final report has to be written with indecent haste.

Where the project involves surveying it is worth taking things step by step, and getting things right before becoming committed to particular questionnaires or interview schedules. There is always a temptation to ignore either the pre-test or the pilot test of a survey instrument. This temptation should be avoided. For pre-testing, send the questionnaire to someone who can evaluate it from the point of view of its contribution to the project. This is usually the supervisor. Send it to someone who can evaluate it as a research tool. This might be the person who was consulted about the research method in the first instance. Also send it to someone who can evaluate it from the point of view of the people who will be supplying the answers. This should provide sufficient comment to enable a second draft to be prepared, which is then piloted by using it to collect information from a few potential respondents. This will show up any operational difficulties, ambiguous questions, and gaps which have previously been overlooked.

The results of the pilot study will enable the survey forms to be finalized and provide some data for testing the coding system and the format of the tables used for the final results. This work often usefully fills the period before the forms are returned.

When designing survey forms it is important, as already noted, to consult a statistician about the size and nature of the sample, and a computer expert about the coding and processing of the results. It is also important to recognize the limitations of the researchers and to avoid becoming swamped by information. This relates to the size of the sample – the number of completed forms that require processing – as well as to the size of the form itself – the number and complexity of the answers. It is always best to err on the cautious side.

As the work progresses, it is important to keep an eye open for trends or consistent patterns. In some cases it is just as important to notice that there are no consistent patterns. The important thing is to remain alert and watch the way things develop. While doing this, retain an open mind. It is easy to jump to conclusions and to start interpreting information in such a way as to reinforce an early suspicion. This is obviously to be avoided.

The other thing to look out for is anything which might suggest a change in the structure of the project. Early results often indicate that something built in as a means of checking is no longer necessary. Alternatively it may prove necessary to add something which would enhance the results. The earlier such changes can be spotted the more chance there is of being able to act upon them.

While attempting to evaluate the results as they come in it is often difficult to retain a clear idea of the shape and purpose of the project. As was noted by one intrepid explorer, 'When you are up to your neck in mud and alligators, it is sometimes difficult to remember that your primary objective is to clear the swamp'. The project supervisor should provide this wider perspective. It is also something that the members of the advisory committee can usually do fairly well. It is worth considering using the advisory committee members as sound-ing-boards for ideas and as a means of checking the relevance of trends and results. This can be done in full committee meetings or through individual contact.

To codify the results and to rehearse arguments it is well worth preparing regular discussion papers on different topics as the research progresses. These can have a number of useful functions. They can reassure the funder that something is actually happening; they can form the basis for discussions in the advisory committee; they can be sent to interested individuals for detailed comment; they help immeasurably to firm up ideas and to put things into context; and, if carefully planned, they can form the basis for different sections of the final report.

As the work progresses the relationship with the supervisor will develop. It is highly likely that there will be periods of tension between the researcher and the supervisor. These should be handled so that they work to the advantage of the research. The tension should be sufficiently creative to encourage the development of new ideas and the exploration of areas where evidence is perhaps a little shaky. The tension should not be such that all constructive communication breaks down. The dividing line is fine and it is not easy to maintain a balance. To do so requires a conscious effort on the part of the supervisor and the researcher.

It is usually easier to maintain this balance if the researcher and the supervisor can let off steam to someone unconnected with the project. This usually means the husband, wife or flat-mate. The contribution which such people have made to research is seldom properly acknowledged.

Feeling lost
About half way through most projects, the research workers experience a period of disillusionment, isolation, frustration and general inertia. This is the time when the researchers feel on the one hand that the problem is so trivial and self-evident that they cannot possibly justify the time spent on the research. This feeling alternates, at fairly short intervals, with the alarming realization that the whole thing is so complex and multi-faceted

114

that it is impossible to do anything more than superficially scrape the surface within the time allowed.

These feelings are quite natural and are experienced by just about every researcher on just about every research project. All that can be done is to keep on going, carry on discussing ideas and work away at the problem. The feeling of isolation and disillusionment will gradually pass and things, usually, seem much clearer as a result.

Reviewing progress

In every project there comes a time when it is necessary to review the progress made and to plan the work for the remainder of the project. This review is often neglected in the hurry to get on with the work. It can, however, make a considerable difference to a project and can ensure that the available resources are used to the best effect.

The scale and nature of the review will obviously vary according to the nature of the research and the size of the project, and several ways of conducting the review have been developed. In all cases, however, the scope of the review will be similar. The review provides an opportunity to pause, to assess what has been achieved and to plan what remains to be done. In this, the proposal plays a vital role. It reminds the researcher of the overall objective and specific aims of the project and should help to put the work back into its proper context.

The best way to begin is to look at what has already been done. The general amount of progress will have implications for the amount of additional work which can be contemplated, while the extent to which specific tasks have been completed will determine the coverage of the remaining research.

The timetable or work schedule in the proposal should indicate whether the rate of progress originally envisaged has been maintained. If it has not, rather than attempting to catch up, it might be more sensible to see whether some of the remaining work could be cut out.

With some projects it is possible to complete discrete aspects of the work and to draw conclusions from them. Where this is so, every effort should be made to write up these pieces of work so that at the review stage their significance for the remainder of the project can be assessed. This is particularly so in projects involving interview surveys or case studies which are examined in turn. After a while it becomes apparent that the main conclusions are consistent, and that all that the remaining interviews or case studies will do is to confirm the earlier findings. When this is the case, it is worth looking closely at the early results to see whether there is anything which requires deeper probing. If not, it may be possible to extend the remainder of the work to cover aspects originally discarded as being beyond the resources available to the project. Alternatively, the project could simply be reduced in size.

Having examined what has so far been achieved, the next stage is to look at what the proposal planned for the remainder of the research project. Perhaps certain aspects could be deleted as unnecessary in the light of early results, or because, as often happens, particularly with lengthy projects, they are overtaken by events. The earlier work will provide a much better understanding of the problem being researched and it should be possible at the review stage to assess whether any change in emphasis is called for. Something may need looking at in greater detail or a new avenue may need to be explored.

The extent to which the remainder of the project can be modified obviously depends on the resources available and the time outstanding. If the project is receiving external funding it may be necessary to involve the funder in the review process. Often funds can be made available at short notice for significant additional work, such as that which might add weight to the conclusions. Alternatively, if reductions in scale are proposed, it might be possible to transfer some of the resources to an alternative purpose, such as dissemination. If there are likely to be changes involving resource allocation, it is as well to involve the funder in the review process as early as possible.

The conduct of the review will mainly be determined by the nature of the project. For some projects, particularly those involving academic research, it may be sufficient to have an extended meeting between the researcher and the supervisor. It is, however, worth the trouble of preparing a paper which can be discussed and which can provide the necessary focus for the decisions that need to be made. Otherwise there is a danger that the meeting will be little more than the regular exchanges between supervisor and researcher, and then the project is in danger of being allowed to drift.

All reviews require a paper of some sort. This can either be the sort of paper described above which attempts to set an agenda for a discussion and to provide a framework for decision-making. More usually the discussion paper will attempt to report the work carried out and to summarize the results, drawing whatever conclusions seem appropriate on the basis of the evidence. Discussion papers often proceed to set out options for further work, or to list alternative courses of action, and in this way to lead the direction of the discussion.

A more detailed version of the discussion paper is the interim report. This has much the same sort of scope but is generally intended for wider dissemination. The primary intention here is to communicate the early results and, often, to promote a discussion of them. This discussion can take place at several different levels. In some instances it is appropriate to discuss the work carried out and the conclusions drawn with the subjects of the research themselves. This is particularly so with some case-study research where the research process is seen as part of a more widely defined change or educational process. In other circumstances it is more appropriate to discuss the interim report with the intended recipients to see whether it meets their needs and if, in the light of the findings, any further aspects require exploration.

Where the project has an advisory committee, the members almost certainly need to be involved in the review process. They are the people who have a reasonably good understanding of what has been going on, while retaining a degree of objectivity. They are in a good position to offer advice on the future direction a project should take.

It is becoming increasingly common to build in a workshop or seminar during the course of the project to review progress and to decide upon future directions. This certainly provides an opportunity to bring together the funding body, the participants, the recipients, members of the advisory committee and other researchers to look closely at the research and to offer advice. Such gatherings are, however, extremely costly in time, money and energy and should only be considered for large research projects where such an investment can be justified. It can also be argued that bringing together such a diverse group of people in fact results in advice that is little better than could be obtained from an advisory committee or similar small meeting.

Whatever form is adopted, the review process should not be overlooked. A single major review is usually sufficient but lengthy projects may require two or three. A formal review should not, of course, obviate the need for the continuous reviewing of the research which should be an integral part of every project.

Finishing up

As the research progresses, more and more attention will focus on the report. If things have proceeded well, much of the difficult thinking will have been done, and it will be a question of drawing the threads together into a coherent whole.

First, stand back from the project, and perhaps go back to the proposal and look again at the overall shape and purpose. This should provide the basis for the shape of the final report. Having decided upon the shape, it is possible then to fit into it any discussion papers produced and to finalize some of the appendices containing the tables of results and so on. It will be a straightforward matter to write the sections describing how the project was carried out. Aim to have a nearly complete report ready before the final results are available.

When it is possible to finalize the report, do so as quickly as possible and send it out for comment. It should probably go to the members of the advisory committee and to a few people closely concerned with the project. The number should be kept fairly small, allowing for a sufficiently wide cross-section of views. On the basis of this round of comments, finalize the report. It is possible to continue to make alterations and to re-draft forever. However, the quality seldom improves much after the second draft.

Now is also the time to be thinking more actively about dissemination. It will by now be apparent whether the results deserve a wide dissemination or whether those who will make

'. . . stand back and look at the overall shape . . .'

use of them can be satisfied by the report alone. It does no one any good to undertake a massive dissemination of the results of a project which is either of limited interest or which was only a limited success. On the other hand, if a project produces interesting results of general interest, much of the value is lost if people are not made aware of them.

A good way to begin dissemination is to use the project address file to notify everyone that the work is completed and that the report will soon be available. In this letter it is usual to summarize the main conclusions and recommendations and indicate any follow-up work. A letter like this also provides an opportunity to thank people for the work they have put into the project. Another successful way of doing this is to hold an open day, to which everyone is invited. It is usually possible to make up some sort of exhibition displaying the results, and there could be two or three papers on the origins of the project, the methods used, the main results and the likely implications. Such an event is an excellent way of rounding off a project and thanking the people who have contributed to it. It is well worth considering.

6

Draw conclusions and make recommendations

This is what everything has been leading up to. Having conducted the research and marshalled all the evidence, the researcher is now faced with the problem of making sense of it all. The information has to be organized, understood and presented in such a way as to allow conclusions to be drawn. The conclusions need to be expressed clearly and unambiguously. From them, recommendations will be made to ensure that some action is taken on the basis of the research. The whole process can be daunting, especially when large amounts of information are involved, but by working methodically and following a number of basic principles the task can be reduced to manageable proportions.

Organize the information
First check the information is complete. There is little point in undertaking a rigorous analysis of complex information only to find that critical parts of it are still being processed by the computing department, or that the results of some of the fieldwork are in a discussion paper produced early in the project and carefully filed away and forgotten.

The preliminary analysis should also be checked. First, to see that it has been completed, and that none is outstanding, and secondly to make sure that the work was done accurately and that, where applicable, all the sums add up. Where necessary,

'. . . check that the information is complete.'

check that all the tests of statistical significance have been carried out.

Statistical information is of little value unless it is accurate, compatible and concerned with comparable events or situations. Accuracy varies. It is greatly affected by the methods used to count and collect the basic statistics. It is always worth checking that the figures have not been rounded up or down, or estimated. Sometimes this is obvious as the figures appear in round hundreds or thousands; what is less obvious is where dubious methods have been used to count the statistics. When statistics have to be counted daily, staff find all sorts of ingenious ways of estimating so as to avoid actually going to the trouble of counting each unit, one by one. If statistics have been compiled in this way they can still be useful, but it is necessary to allow for some inaccuracy.

Compatibility is important when comparing statistics. The statistics should be compiled using the same definitions, they should relate to the same time periods and should be counted in the same manner. It is possible to use data which are not strictly compatible, but when doing so it is necessary to make due allowances. More important is the need to check that everything is understood. Where information is qualified, this should be noted, and it should be clear what the qualifications imply. Similarly the significance of things like the fact that information was collected at different times of the year should be noted. It should also be possible to understand the relationships between the types of information collected, which might require looking again at the proposal to see exactly why each set of information was collected. With small projects all of this can be done quite quickly and easily but with larger studies this careful organization and verification can take some time. It will, however, be time well spent.

It is usually possible with small projects to absorb and retain most of the information and to think things through, arranging and re-arranging the evidence within the confines of the human mind. This is not possible with larger projects, and here the aim must be to retain a sort of mental map of the information, so that each element of significance can be retrieved selectively.

Having charted a course through the evidence, the next stage is to sift and consider. It helps to have the information immediately to hand and many people find that the best way to do it is to spread everything out over the office floor and to absorb the evidence by osmosis. Others find a more conventional pose more suitable.

Analyse the information
This is not easy. It is necessary to have a clear mind and a sharp eye to pick up the unusual or to spot a pattern or a trend. It is almost like detective work in the Sherlock Holmes tradition – a process of looking for clues and interpreting them to arrive at conclusions.

It is best to begin by knowing what to look for. Go back to the objective of the research and to the specific aims. If relevant, return to the hypothesis. These should provide the starting point and indicate the direction that the search should take. They also help to determine the significance of each piece of evidence. It is then necessary to work slowly and methodically through the evidence, looking for anything that supports or negates the hypothesis or is relevant to the objective or aims. The researcher is looking for patterns and consistency in the information. Sometimes these are reflected as discernible trends which can provide support or contradiction. In some instances it is the very fact that there is no pattern that is significant. In such cases the researcher is looking for the odd one out. This is the usual pattern when analysing tables of statistics, taking each line at a time and then each column, scanning the figures for consistency, for rising or declining trends and for anomalies. This is a skill which, with practice, can soon be developed, and can prove invaluable in making sense of large amounts of statistical information. In looking at the evidence in this way, try to work out what is happening, what exactly the evidence illustrates. Above all, try to *understand* rather than just process data.

There are several traps to avoid. First of all, avoid non-existent causal relationships. When two things which could be related demonstrate similar trends or patterns there is a temptation to deduce that one trend is caused by the other. This may be the case, but usually much more evidence is required. As was noted

'. . . detective work in the Sherlock Holmes tradition . . .'

earlier, since the 1950s there has been a nearly identical growth in the rise of juvenile delinquency and in the use of ball-point pens. The two events are unlikely to be linked by a causal relationship, even though they may both be products of the rise of the consumer society. When spotting similar trends or patterns, it is usually sufficient at this stage to note that there seems to be some sort of relationship which may be illuminated by further information.

Even where events are related, the nature of the relationship may be obscure. A change in one variable is seldom caused solely by changes in one other. More commonly there are several variables which together cause changes, and in looking in turn at the relationships between single variables the true picture is obscured. In such cases it is necessary to look at things in the round – to try to see all the different facets before coming to a conclusion.

In other instances the very process of aggregation can hide things of significance. This is often the case with statisticalicformation, particularly when it comes to information containing proportions and percentages. A case in point occurred some years ago when, despite a high general rate of inflation, it appeared that the average price of books was falling. This surprised many people concerned with buying books as all their evidence pointed to quite large increases in the average prices of different types of book. Table 2 shows what was happening.

TABLE 2. The average prices of books

Category of book	Year one		Year two		Percentage change	
	Average price	Number published	Average price	Number published	Average price	Number published
Fiction	£4.00	500	£4.50	800	+12.5%	+60%
Junior	£2.00	400	£2.25	550	+12.5%	+37.5%
Non-fiction	£8.00	1000	£9.00	750	+12.5%	−25%
Total	£5.68	1900	£5.52	2100	−2.8%	+10.5%

The average price of books within each category rises by 12.5% from year one to year two, yet the total registers a drop of 2.8%. The reason for this is that the proportions of different types of book changed between the two years. In year two a smaller proportion of expensive non-fiction books was published and this had the effect of lowering the overall average price. It is always worth being aware of situations like this and taking care to use disaggregated information whenever possible.

When analysing the results of interviews or questionnaires completed by members of the public, it is important to make allowances for the different life experiences of different groups. For example, people born before the First World War have experienced two major wars and the Depression. They have received few of the benefits of the welfare state. It is not surprising that their outlook on life is likely to be rather different from that of someone born immediately after the Second World War. Due allowances for these different outlooks on life should always be made when looking at information that sets out to portray different satisfaction levels for different age-groups of people.

Above all else it is important to avoid the trap of making more of the results than can be justified by the evidence. If the evidence is slender, do not try to strengthen it artificially. It is, of course, always necessary to look for supporting evidence and to reinforce findings with other facts; that is quite a different matter.

Finally, having sifted all the evidence and noted all that is noteworthy, consider whether any additional information would be useful. It may not be possible to collect such information for the purposes of the project in hand but it may be desirable to recommend that such information should be collected in the future.

Draw the conclusions
Taking each of the specific aims of the project, set down the conclusions that apply to each one. For every conclusion ask the question 'Is it really reasonable to conclude that on the evidence available?' If it is, the conclusion can stand as it is. If not, it will probably be necessary to add a qualifying phrase.

When drawing conclusions, researchers should be aware that they have, by this stage, probably looked more closely at the problem than most other people. They are therefore in a position to make subjective comments which should carry some weight. If the evidence for a particular conclusion is lacking, but the researcher is confident in making the conclusion all the same, it is worth reinforcing it with a relevant phrase, such as 'While not entirely borne out by the evidence, the researcher did feel this to be the case.'

Set out all the positive evidence and conclusions, then go back and play devil's advocate, attempting to disprove the conclusions. Where necessary, qualify the conclusion in the light of any contradictory evidence. Having settled on the main conclusions, try to look at them as a whole to see whether there are any internal contradictions. Consider whether this is because of contradictory evidence, or simply a case of poor drafting. Finally, look at each conclusion in turn to check that the drafting expresses the conclusion concisely and precisely.

Make recommendations
A recommendation is simply a suggestion to someone to do something. Recommendations should flow logically from the conclusions of the research and should be carefully drafted to ensure that the right person or body takes the right action about the right thing.

Wherever possible, recommendations should be precise. Detail is seldom necessary, precision always so. However, it is not always possible to be extremely precise, indeed the very purpose of the recommendation may be to clear up confusion surrounding a subject. In such cases the recommendation should reflect this uncertainty. In other instances, the practicalities of undertaking the action may be uncertain and the recommendation again needs to reflect this.

These degrees of specificity can best be illustrated by an example. Suppose that a research project in a public library has produced the conclusion that 'bookstock management policies were impaired by a general lack of information about book purchases and allocation.' This could give rise to a general recommendation:

Statistics of book purchase and allocation should be improved.

This covers the point but is rather vague and could easily

become lost or forgotten. It could be sharpened considerably by directing it at whoever would be responsible for taking the action:

The senior management team should improve the statistical information about book purchase and allocation.

This targets the recommendation, and makes it less easily ignored. It still does not indicate why the information needs to be improved. To do this it might be worth adding another phrase:

The senior management team should improve the statistical information about book purchase and allocation in order to assist the implementation of bookstock management policies.

Even this does not indicate the ways in which the statistics are deficient and need improvement. If the senior management team is unlikely to spot these ways quickly, the recommendation should point the way for them:

The senior management team should improve the accuracy, compatibility and currency of statistics about the allocation and purchase of books in order to assist the implementation of bookstock management policies.

This makes things very specific and allows little room for manoeuvre on the part of the senior management team. This may not be tactically appropriate, in which case it might be best to forget the specificity and simply include something that calls for action and implies an element of accountability while leaving the interpretation open:

The senior management team should give full consideration to the need for management information in connection with the implementation of bookstock management policies.

Note the use of 'management information' rather than 'statistical information – getting the jargon and terminology right is just as important as the content.

It is all a question of aiming the recommendations in the right direction and expressing them in the most appropriate format. Once the initial draft of the recommendations has been produced it is worth reading them from the point of view of the recipient and redrafting accordingly.

7
Write the report

No research project is complete without a report. Unless some form of report is made, the only people to benefit from the work are the researchers.

The nature of the report is determined by the project itself and the audience to which the report is addressed. Short projects carried out at the request of a senior management team, for example, might simply be reported by means of a brief paper supported by an oral presentation. Academic research, on the other hand, is expected to produce lengthy reports, or theses, covering all aspects of the research and reporting on them in a precise and rather formal manner. Between these two extremes there is considerable variety.

No matter what the size or formality of the report, it is reasonable to expect it to convey information on a fairly standard set of topics. First it must say why the work was done, what events led up to it and what other work was found to be relevant. This is usually contained in the introduction, which should also include the precise statement of the objective and aims of the project.

There should be a section describing what work was done. This should cover the methods used, their selection and any problems experienced in their application. From this it is easy to move on to what was found out, or the results. In turn, these lead on to the conclusions, which are a statement of what the researcher deduced from the results, and then on to the recommendations which set out what the researcher feels should be the action taken as a result of the conclusions.

In academic reports it is customary to include a section between the conclusions and recommendations to provide a discussion of the results and conclusions. In a formal sense this is the correct sequence as the conclusions need to be drawn solely on the basis of the results, but they can then be supplemented by the general experience and impressions of the researcher, as set out in the discussion section. All this is then followed by recommendations. This arrangement may be appropriate in formal academic work but for other purposes much impact can be lost by separating the results from the discussion, and increasingly it is acceptable to have a results section that contains both the factual results – what was obtained by analysing the information – and the discussion of their significance – which is obtained by interpreting the results. As with so many things, the final decision must be a matter for common sense and an understanding of the audience to whom the report is addressed.

The introduction

This provides the general background to the work. It should set the context within which everything that follows needs to be considered. It should provide a brief historical introduction and should relate this to any other relevant research or developmental work. Rather more detail should be given on the reasons for the project, any specific events that led up to it, or the nature of the problems that precipitated it.

The introduction should then set out the purpose of the research, specifying the objective and the aims, and listing any hypotheses that were to be tested. In certain circumstances it might be necessary to qualify this by indicating the scope of the project, any limitations imposed, or any steps taken to make the task more manageable. Finally, the introduction is the place for any mention of sources of finance for the research and for acknowledging the help received during the research.

Methods

This section should begin with a description of the overall design of the research, putting each of the methods into its proper context and highlighting the relationships between them. Each method should then be described in turn, noting how it was developed or modified to meet specific needs. For surveys it is important to cover such points as the size of the population surveyed, the sampling frame used and the size and nature of the sample.

The section should go on to describe how the methods were used. This includes the sequence of events during the project, showing how the methods fitted into each other and how the work progressed. Any problems experienced should be mentioned and discussed as these may have implications for the results and are certainly of interest to anyone wishing to use the methods for a similar purpose. There should be a description of how the information was analysed, again noting any problems which arose.

Depending on the audience for the report, it may be worth including copies of any forms, questionnaires, schedules and so on that were used during the course of the project. These should almost always be included as appendices to the main report.

Results

The formality of the report conditions the approach to be adopted here. The more academic the work, the more precise must be the specification of the results. There should be little interpretation and little room for selecting the most significant results and highlighting them while giving less prominence to those which contributed less to the project. In other reports there is more scope for interpretation and emphasis.

In theory, if the research design is appropriate, all the results will be relevant. In practice this is seldom so, and the results of some of the analyses contribute little to the project. In such cases it may be worth noting that the analyses took place but did not really lead anywhere. It is probably not worth including all the resulting tables.

In formal reports the results should appear with a brief introduction and a brief commentary on each. This is easy when the results appear in the form of tables, as after a questionnaire survey. It is, however, a style less suited to qualitative types of research where the results may be contained in a discursive narrative. In such cases the form of the results should determine the presentation. Certainly, from the point of view of a reader, a discursive narrative is easier to handle than a series of what can easily appear as disjointed statements.

Similarly, the question of whether to include the discussion of the results in this section should be determined by the nature of the results and the audience. It is also a matter of taste, but reports that combine results and discussion do appear to provide a more rounded summary of the research.

The discussion should provide an element of interpretation of the results, perhaps deducing things from them – 'If the results show X, Y and Z, it follows that. . .' It is sometimes possible to predict future events on the basis of the results – 'If A, B and C have happened in the past, it is likely that in future. . .' Whenever interpretation is made on the basis of the results it should be clearly indicated as such. Failure to do this can cause all sorts of confusion about what exactly are results and what are interpretations.

Conclusions

In a good report the conclusions flow smoothly from the results. They can be presented as a simple list but it is much better to place them in a narrative, emphasizing the exact statement by typographical means – underlining, italicizing or indenting. The conclusions should be concisely and precisely phrased and should cover only that which they are intended to cover. Some care needs to be taken with the drafting to ensure this.

Just as the results can be interpreted, so it is possible to qualify the conclusions by adding the subjective impressions gained from participating in the research project. This point has been covered in the previous section and it should be sufficient to note it here. Some research reports include in the conclusions section a review of the project as a whole, which attempts to assess the overall success and the appropriateness of the methods used.

Discussion
This is the place in the sequence for the discussion of results in formal academic reports or theses.

Recommendations
This is the most important part of the report for some projects. It is an attempt to recommend action which should be taken as a result of the findings of the research. In what might be termed 'management reports' it is often customary to include a summary of recommendations at the front of the report so that potential readers can judge whether it is worth going to the trouble of reading the whole report. Of course, the danger of this is that people only read the recommendations and act upon them without being aware of the background to them. Where such summaries are called for, it is far better to write a summary including the recommendations and putting them into context.

Every research project is a contribution towards increasing our understanding of the world around us. As such it is customary to include a recommendation about further research. This is often seen as an attempt by researchers to ensure a continuing flow of work for themselves. A more charitable interpretation would be that the researcher, having concluded the work and being fully aware of the deficiencies, is in the best position to indicate the most effective way of developing our understanding in that particular area.

Style
When asked about style, Matthew Arnold is reputed to have replied: 'People think I can teach them style. What stuff it is. Have something to say and say it as clearly as you can. That is the only secret of style.' That was quoted in *Writing plain English* which does in fact go some way towards helping people to say things as clearly as they can. From the book it is possible to select ten lessons which should be considered by researchers faced with the task of writing the research report.

1 *Do not assume prior knowledge*
As the researcher, you will be writing the report having spent considerable time studying the problem. The readers of the

reports will not be in that position and you should take care to avoid assuming that certain things are self-evident.

2 *Write as if explaining the points to a panel of readers sitting opposite*

Try to avoid over-formal presentations. These may be thought to be required in some forms of academic theses, but often it is possible to adopt a style which avoids the stiffness certain formality can produce. At the same time, avoid falling into the trap of being patronizing. Remember that the readers are 'sitting opposite' and do not like being talked down to.

3 *Try to 'sell' the information*

After all that research it is worth making the effort to communicate the information in the most effective way. This usually means writing to convince and to interest. Too many reports are dry and dull with no spark to encourage interest from the reader.

4 *Choose words learnt early in life*

For erroneous, use wrong; for endeavour, use try; for implement, use do; for necessitate, use need, and for terminate, use end. Little is served by using long and complex words. Only occasionally does the exact meaning of a sentence or phrase call for their use. When in doubt use the shorter word; this is usually one derived from the Anglo-Saxon root as opposed to a Latin or Greek root.

5 *Keep sentences short and simple*

It is reasonable to aim for an average length of about 20 words. On the whole, shorter sentences are more easily understood. They can, however, become rather boring, and it is worth trying to vary the length a little. Avoid reducing the sentences by leaving out important words like 'a', 'the' and 'that'. To do so can make sentences ambiguous as can be seen from this bewildering example found in a public library.

Books for lending around the walls, those for reference on island book-cases.

'Choose words learnt early in life'

Aim to construct sentences simply. Where sub-clauses are necessary, use them sparingly and avoid having more than two in any single sentence.

6   *Use the active tense rather than the passive*
It simply sounds more positive than 'the active tense should always be used in preference to the passive'.

7   *Break down complicated ideas into separate parts*
It is not always easy to express an idea or concept simply in a single sentence. Some concepts are just not that simple. In such cases, look at ways of breaking up the statement into different parts. It might even be worth setting them out as numbered sections.

8   *Keep to basic punctuation*
The staple diet should be full-stops and commas. Semi-colons can be tricky except when used to separate phrases which appear as a list. Dashes and brackets can be effective but only if used sparingly.

9   *Aim to get it right first time*
It is always worth aiming to produce the final version at the first attempt. To write with the idea that what is written will be re-drafted encourages a degree of carelessness which can produce drafts which require complete revision. On the other hand, if the aim is to get it right first time there is every chance that all that will be required is minor amendment. This is as much an attitude of mind as a matter of style. Use word processors at your peril.

10   *Test it for readability*
The following test has been developed from R. Gunning's FOG (Frequency of gobbledygook) formula by the Plain English Campaign.

- Count a 100-word sample.
- Count the number of complete sentences in the sample. Count the total number of words in the complete sentences.

Divide the number of words by the number of sentences. This gives the average sentence length.

- Count the number of words with three or more syllables in the 100 words. This gives the percentage of long words in the sample.

- Add the average sentence length to the percentage of long words to give the test score.

- Repeat the process twice and average the test scores. This gives the final FOG score.

For comparison, tests carried out in 1980 by the National Consumer Council showed that the following publications had these FOG scores:

Woman	25
The Sun	25
Daily Mail	31
The Times	36
The Guardian	39

It is hard to admit, but the manuscript for this book has a FOG score of about 42. It should be possible to do better than this in any research report.

If you want to read more about report writing, I recommend Nick Moore and Martin Hesp, *The basics of writing reports, etc.*, Bingley, 1985.

8

Disseminate the results

The value of any completed research is latent and requires dissemination to make it active. A research project which discovered the cure for cancer would be immensely valuable but that value would only be realized, or released, when the results of the research were communicated to those who could make use of them.

Dissemination is the process of communicating information about a research project to the those people and organizations which require the information. The art of good dissemination lies in selecting the form which best suits both the research and the potential audience. It does not take place only after the research has been completed. In good projects, dissemination begins at the outset of the work when information about the existence of the project is communicated to those who make up the potential audience for the results. During the project there should be a continuous flow of information about the project. Detailed information will be requested by researchers in related fields, information required by the funder, current awareness information needed for the community at large, and perhaps even news releases through local papers to inform members of the public about the work. All of this contributes towards the creation of an informed environment into which the results, conclusions and recommendations will be released. This process of creating awareness of the project is extremely important, but often overlooked.

The audience for any research project is made up of three groups. Most obvious are those actively awaiting the conclusion of the project. They want to see the complete final report and wish to consider, in some detail, the results, conclusions and recommendations. It is not difficult to dissiminate to this group. They are usually fairly easy to identify and are content with the final report of the project. It will not be necessary to 'sell' the project to them but simply to ensure that the report is in the format which will best communicate the results to them. For any single research project, this group is never likely to be very large.

The next most significant group is those who will find something of interest or value in the research, but would not automatically seek a copy of the final report. It will be necessary to stimulate the interest of this group by 'selling' the report to them and encouraging them to consider the results, conclusions and recommendations. Once the significance of the report is indicated, this group will probably want a fair amount of detail, perhaps as much as those in the first group. Their interest in the research is also latent.

The third group is those who want to know of the existence of the work and probably want to know something of the main findings and recommendations but, beyond that, they have little interest at present. At some time in the future, their interest may grow, in which case they need to be able to obtain access to fuller information but for the moment the bare bones will be sufficient.

The aims of any dissemination exercise should be to alert the last group to the existence of the research; to provide the second group with an interesting summary and a means of obtaining fuller information; and to give the first group the full results, conclusions and recommendations and to provide them with an opportunity to discuss them.

For the most effective dissemination it is necessary to plan a campaign if the greatest impact is to be achieved. The techniques used vary according to the nature of the work and the type of audience, and the whole process will take place over a long time.

General announcements
The best way to begin is with a press release. This can be sent to all the relevant journals, and with careful drafting the same release can meet the needs of the popular journals and those, more scholarly ones, which contain announcements about the research. With luck, the same press release can accompany review copies of any published report.

The press release should begin with a snappy, eyecatching sentence which will both encourage editors to include the item and readers to read it. The whole release should run to no more than one A4 page of typescript, yet should encapsulate the research. To make life even more difficult, it should be written so that an editor can cut if after the first paragraph without losing any of the sense of the piece. It can be done but needs practice and, for the inexperienced, it is worth consulting a public relations officer. That vital first paragraph should indicate the coverage of the research; the most significant findings and any relevant recommendations; and an indication of where further information can be obtained. (There is a chapter on press releases in *The basics of writing reports, etc.*)

This should ensure coverage in most of the journals scanned by those in the third group. It will also, however, be necessary to obtain a mention in abstracting and indexing journals. The press release is usually sufficient for this. Occasionally one of the journals will ask for a copy of the report, but a good press release should be sufficient for most purposes.

Stimulating interest
The aim here is to provide an interesting summary for those who need to know about the research but who do not yet know that they need to know. It has to be something which will stimulate their interest and whet their appetite for more. The most effective vehicle here is probably a journal article. The benefits of this are that an article reaches a wide selection of people; it is relatively permanent and transmittable; it is an accepted means of keeping up-to-date and finding out about

what is going on; and finally, journal articles are covered by indexing and abstracting services, so it is possible to reinforce an earlier mention.

It is important to select the journals most likely to be read by the target audience. There is likely to be a range of these and it is probably worth approaching their editors to see whether they are interested in an article and when it would be likely to appear. It is then a matter of writing an article to suit the requirements of a particular journal. It is not usually sensible to produce two very similar articles for similar journals – they are, anyway, likely to be read by the same people – it is better to go for one serious journal and another which is more popular.

This second group of potential consumers of the research may be prepared to purchase a summary, or popularized version, of the full report. This is often the case when the research is relevant to a homogeneous group of organizations, such as universities or local-authority departments. Organizations such as these can afford to purchase reports and are used to handling them. If there appears to be a market for reports of this nature, they are well worth considering. They are durable, they provide more room for discussion of the results and they are likely to make more impact than a single journal article. There does, however, need to be a fair degree of certainty that the report will sell to justify the expense involved in re-writing in a more popular, summary style, and in publication.

Conferences are good places for stimulating people's interest in research projects. There is a growing number of conferences that involve a general call for papers. It is then open to anyone to submit an outline paper to the conference organizers. Such conferences often turn out to be unwieldy affairs, with many papers but little cohesion. They do, however, provide a means of announcing the existence of the research and providing a summary of the findings. Increasingly, to cope with the large numbers of papers submitted, these open conferences have what are known as poster sessions. These can be very effective for getting information across to people who have more than just a general interest. Basically, the idea is that the person or organization which wants to communicate something, instead of preparing a conference paper, prepares a poster or display conveying the essence of the research. They then make themselves available at scheduled times for interested people to go along and discuss the work in detail. This opportunity for personal discussion can prove very valuable but, of course, only a few people can be handled at any one time.

Conferences which are built around a theme and in which the speakers are selected by the organizers are usually more succesful than the free-for-alls. It is worth keeping an eye open for forthcoming conferences on subjects relevant to the research. It may seem rather impertinent to contact the conference organizer to offer to give a paper, but frequently the organizer is only too pleased to include some current research.

Preaching to the converted

This is the most straightforward group to reach. The main question conditioning the form of dissemination concerns the size of the group. Most particularly, is this group, combined with those whose interest can be stimulated, sufficient to justify full publication of the report? If the answer is no, this does not mean that nothing should happen. The group still needs to know about the research and it is often justifiable to distribute copies of the final report to those interested, inviting any others to apply for a copy. The means of reproduction and distribution are chosen on grounds of cost and, while the end product might not be aesthetically wonderful, the information will at least, have been communicated.

The larger the group, the more time and effort can be justifiably spent on the production and publication of the final report. If the market is sufficiently large to justify commercial publication, it will almost certainly justify substantial editing or even re-drafting to transform it from a research report into a book.

Whether commercial publication is chosen, or copies are simply sent to interested parties, it is worth ensuring that copies are available from appropriate libraries so that those who might later wish to gain access to the report can do so.

Having communicated the information to those who want it, it is often worth providing an opportunity for them to get together to discuss the matter. If it is a small group, it is not difficult to convene a meeting, inviting all the interested parties.

144

Alternatively, it might be worth organizing a workshop, seminar or conference, depending on the size of the group and the nature of the research. It is worth allowing some time for people to obtain the report and to digest it before organizing the meeting. The only exception to this is where a meeting is called when the results of the research have been established but it is felt that a general discussion would be useful before finalizing the report. This usually results in a very authoritative report and ensures a high degree of commitment by the participants.

Dissemination is considered most at the end of the research. There is, therefore, a tendency to pay it only scant attention. After all, the main work has been completed, and thoughts are moving on to other things. It should not be overlooked, however. Not only is it essential in the general transmission of ideas and the collective growth of knowledge and understanding, but it can also be the most rewarding part of the research as it provides an opportunity to discuss ideas with other interested people and to gain the maximum value from the research process as a whole.

Good dissemination should be regarded as the essential end of a research project. It can be achieved relatively easily. Like most other things to do with research, it is simply a matter of common sense.

'Good dissemination . . .'

9

Further reading

There is much literature on research and research techniques but most of it is very technical and written with the needs of professional researchers in mind. The books listed here are, on the whole, intended for people who are relatively inexperienced in research.

1   Centre for Research on User Studies *CRUS Guides*, University of Sheffield, 1984–5.
    1. *Designing a user study: general research design*
    2. *Basic social research techniques*
    3. *Analysing data*
    4. *Writing research reports*
    5. *Questionnaires*
    6. *Interviews*
    7. *Observation*
    8. *Group decision techniques*
    9. *Community profiling*
    10. *Group interviewing*
A very practical set of guides.

2   Gardner, Godfrey *Social surveys for social planners*, Milton Keynes, Open University Press, 1978.
    This is good on social survey techniques and readable and comprehensive. One of the best books on survey methodology.

3   Hedley, Rodney *Measuring success: a guide to evaluation for*

voluntary and community groups, Neighbourhood Care Action Programme, 1985.

This is a good, basic guide, which is aimed at voluntary and community groups but has a much wider significance.

4   Hoinville, Gerald and Jowell, Roger, and Associates, *Survey research practice*, Heinemann Educational Books, 1978.

The book deals with all stages of the survey, from the initial planning to the production of 'clean' data. Based on the collective experience of researchers working at Social and Community Planning Research, the book is detailed without being too technical.

5   Maher, Chrissie and Cutts, Martin, *Writing plain English*, Manchester, Plain English Campaign, 1980.

This is an invaluable guide to the art of writing simply and effectively, based on the authors' experience of writing and designing forms, leaflets and other material. It will be of use when writing the research report and earlier for questionnaire design.

6   Moore, Nick and Hesp, Martin, *The basics of writing reports, etc.*, Bingley, 1985.

Intended as a practical, down-to-earth guide to writing and presenting reports of all kinds, this book has a chapter devoted to the production of research reports. Also relevant are the chapters on press releases, presenting statistical information, writing clearly and the use of printers. Perhaps not surprisingly, I can recommend it whole heartedly.

7   Moroney, M. J., *Facts from figures*, Harmondsworth, Penguin Books 1975.

This is probably the best basic text on statistics. It is a bit heavy to wade through in places but is invaluable as a reference source and a means of checking statistical techniques.

8   Stacey, Margaret, *Methods of social research*, Oxford, Pergamon, 1969.

This is a standard text. It is rather technical and a little wordy, but it is very thorough.

Index